THE ART OF ANCIENT SYRIA

PRE-ISLAMIC MONUMENTS
OF THE
SYRIAN ARAB REPUBLIC

HORST KLENGEL

The Art of Ancient SYRIA

SOUTH BRUNSWICK AND NEW YORK:
A.S. BARNES AND COMPANY
LONDON: THOMAS YOSELOFF LTD

Translated from the German by Joan Becker

English Language edition
© 1972 by A. S. Barnes and Co., Inc.
German copyright 1971 by Edition Leipzig
A. S. Barnes and Co., Inc.
Cranbury, New Jersey 08512
Thomas Yoseloff Ltd
108 New Bond Street
London W1Y OQX, England
Library of Congress Catalog Card Number 72–6062
Printed in the German Democratic Republic

CONTENTS

INTRODUCTION

The region now within the frontiers of the Syrian Arab Republic has one of the oldest cultures in the world. Archaeological and historical research has revealed this with increasing clarity in the course of recent decades, and our knowledge of the pre-Islamic cultures which flourished here and the fate of the people who created and represented them gains scope, accuracy and colour year by year. The results of the work done by Syrian and foreign expeditions fit together like the stones in a mosaic to form an increasingly complete and informative picture.

A steadily growing number of people are engaged in throwing light on the ancient history of Syria and, in view of the current importance of its cultural heritage, the government of the Syrian Arab Republic devotes considerable attention to archaeological research. The Department of Ancient Monuments and Museums is doing magnificent work in excavating, preserving and re-constructing what was created in long-past centuries, and scholars from all over the world, who are finding answers to questions of the origin of their own cultures here, are assisting them in this work. One of the main aims of this book, too, is to win friends for Syria and its ancient history.

The Department of Ancient Monuments and Museums of the Syrian Arab Republic gave generous and friendly assistance in the preparation of this illustrated volume, which is intended to give an impression of the most important Syrian ruins of the pre-Islamic period. We owe especially cordial thanks to Director-General Abdul-Hamid Darkal and his colleagues Adnan Bounni, Bekhir Zouhdi, Kassem Toueir and Marwan Musselmani, to Khaled Ass'ad, Director of the Museum of Palmyra, and Shawqi Shaath, Director of the Museum of Aleppo. The author also wishes to thank all those who showed him the well-known Arab hospitality during his visits in the Syrian Arab Republic. Thanks are also due to Professor Paolo Matthiae, in charge of Italian excavations at Tell Mardikh, for his kind provision and designation of photographs.

There are so many relics of pre-Islamic times in the Syrian Arab Republic that several volumes would be needed to illustrate them in anything like completeness. It was therefore necessary to concentrate on a few important and characteristic ancient Syrian sites and to give an impression of what these ancient monuments look like today. For this reason they are not presented in a chronological order or context of style, but according to where they are situated. There are some additional photographs of isolated finds now to be seen in museums of the Syrian Arab Republic. In the foreground stands the architectural monument in its natural surroundings, the beautiful and varied landscape of Syria. Excavation or reconstruction work is now going on in almost all the places shown in this book. The picture which can now be presented —mainly of the situation in Spring 1969—will therefore change to a greater or lesser degree in future.

TIME AND SPACE

In view of the cultural and historical development of the country, the term "Syrian Arab Republic" is both an expansion and a limitation compared with the term "Syria". On the one hand, parts of Mesopotamia, i.e., regions between the Tigris and the Euphrates, which did not belong to ancient Syria, are within the frontiers of the Syrian Arab Republic, while on the other hand a restriction to this territory excludes those parts of ancient Syria in the north and southwest which are now Turkish or form part of the Republic of Lebanon.

The term "pre-Islamic times" here includes a whole series of historical periods each with its own cultural features. The beginnings are still unclear, but discoveries have been made in caves which show that hunters and collectors of plants already lived in Syria in the Early Stone Age. Discoveries on a large number of sites make it possible to trace the subsequent developments which led to settled farming during the so-called Neolithic revolution. But inscriptions—the evidence which makes historical events and persons understandable—are lacking until well into the 3rd millennium. When the first written information appeared—first in the more highly developed countries on the Euphrates and Nile—Syria had already advanced far into the Bronze Age and had in many places completed the transition to class society, the early stage of which we shall here call "ancient oriental". The Graeco-Roman period follows and Palmyra succeeded in gaining a special position within it. This merges without any sharp break into the Eastern Roman Byzantine period which lies between antiquit y and Islam. Exact dates can hardly be given for these periods, since the changes which ushered in a new epoch in the development of Syria were socio-economic processes which cannot be determined by dates. Changes also often occurred at different times and in different ways in the various parts of Syria. Nevertheless, for the sake of clarity, a few dates connected with political and military matters will be given here: the Ancient Oriental period dates from about 2500 to 333 B.C. (Alexander the Great); the Graeco-Roman period from 333 B.C. to 395 A.D. (division of the Roman Empire); the Eastern-Roman Byzantine Period from 395 to 635 A.D. (conquest of Damascus by the Moslem Arabs). Palmyra, the caravan city in the heart of the Syrian desert, flourished in the 2nd and 3rd centuries A.D., that is, in the period of Roman rule in the eastern Mediterranean.

Knowledge of its natural conditions—climate and vegetation, the nature of the soil and landscape—is always an important key to a better understanding of the cultural and historical development of a country and of its special features. The farther back we look in history the more fully must we take into account the environmental factors with which man had to contend in his search for a livelihood.

A great part of the Syrian Arab Republic is within the so-called fertile crescent, the region stretching in a broad semi-circle open to the south from the Persian Gulf through Upper Mesopotamia and northern Syria to Palestine which has sufficient rainfall. The line linking places which have an annual average rainfall of 250 mm can be regarded as the frontier line for continuous and fruitful farming, but man's creative ability and a favourable surface relief have often resulted in this line being broken through. Irrigation by means of raising the level of river waters with the help of various technical devices and conducting it into the fields through a network of canals has never played an important part in Syria, farming on the basis of rainfall

remained predominant. The grazing zone bordering on the farming land, which has an average annual rainfall of less than 250 mm but more than 100 mm, produces lush grasses and weeds after the winter rains and provides plenty of fodder for flocks; in late spring, however, it dries up quickly as the sun rises higher and shepherds and goatherds move with their flocks to the edge of the farming lands. South of the mountain ridges which stretch from the Euphrates via Palmyra to the southwest as far as Damascus, the land changes more and more into desert. The advent of the camel first opened up the desert to man.

If we look at the most important landscape zones of the Syrian Arab Republic in an east-westerly direction, we first see the coast with its natural harbours; of these Ras Shamra (Ugarit), Latakia (Laodicea), Djeble (Gabala) and Ruad (Arwad) in particular played a role in trade. The mountains which follow the Levantine coast and shut it off from the interior gradually retreat inland in the north and considerably decrease in height, so that the Syrian harbours had a broad hinterland made fruitful by abundant rainfall and were also more easily accessible from the hinterland. We can deduce from inscriptions that the coastal mountains were much more thickly wooded in ancient times than they are today; this natural wealth has been decimated by long years of indiscriminate deforestation and grazing. Farming was possible in the escarpment zone linking up with the coastal mountains to the east, through which the Afrin and the Nahr el-'Assi (Orontes) flow. Farther to the east the Central and North Syrian hill country leads into the fertile valleys round Haleb—Aleppo and Homs;

there is evidence from the earliest times that these were corn-growing regions. Another good farming region lies in the south of the Syrian Arab Republic, in the Hauran. The oasis of Damascus, the Ghuta, became increasingly important after the 2nd millennium. These agricultural regions, which were even able to export their products, are all-too-often immediately followed by desert in the east, where man can live permanently only at a few ground-water oases. On the Euphrates the desert plateau descends fairly steeply to the river valley, in which sufficient land could be irrigated by a simple system of canals to provide space for towns like Mari and Dura Europos. The grazing land of the Djezire ("Island") begins on the other side of the Euphrates; the rivers Belikh and Khabur flow through this region and to the north it merges into the rainwater-farming zone. These natural conditions greatly influenced the historical development of ancient Syria. Since watering-places were rare south of Palmyra and often dried up completely, trade caravans were forced to détour far to the north on their way from southern Mesopotamia to the west. So long as the donkey was the customary beast of burden, two routes were especially important: the route which followed the Euphrates to the north as far as Meskene and then turned off towards Haleb (formerly Khalab), which probably corresponded approximately to the present motor road from Der es-Zor to Haleb, and a southerly route which left the Euphrates at about the position of Mari and Dura Europos and reached the cultivated regions of Syria via Palmyra. The introduction of the camel as the caravans' main beast of burden opened up new possibilities of crossing the desert, since the camel can exist for a long time without water. The route from Bosra to the Persian Gulf now gained in importance. In Roman times the already existing network of roads was much extended.

Syria was thus drawn into the trade of the ancient world, not only transporting goods but also taking an active part in trade with its own products, especially agricultural products and products of its highly developed handicrafts. Archaeological investigations in pre-Islamic settlements have clearly shown the extent to which a number of places were able to profit by trade.

PRE-ISLAMIC POLITICAL DEVELOPMENTS

Syria's position as a bridge between East and West, and also its favourable natural conditions, encouraged economic development. Its culture constantly received new impulses from outside, mainly through trade; these were eagerly accepted, further developed and merged with the already existing culture. But the above-mentioned conditions had negative effects on the political development of the country; they encouraged polycentrism, the existence of smaller states side by side and opposed to each other which could only be forced to join up into larger units under pressure from without— from the Egyptians, Hittites, Assyrians, Persians and Romans, for example. The kingdoms of Mari, Yamkhad (round Haleb-Aleppo) and Qatna (el-Mishrife near Homs), which were important in the 2nd millennium B.C., were as little able to dominate the whole of Syria as Ugarit. The origin and centre of the kingdom of Mitanni, which flourished in the middle of the 2nd millennium, was in Upper Mesopotamia. In the 1st millennium B.C. the Aramaic kingdoms of Hamath (Hama) and Aram-Damascus succeeded in playing a greater role and gathering around them a number of Syrian states and tribes in the struggle against Assyrian expansion. Later on a number of Arab states on the borders of the cultivated region gained importance and Palmyra even succeeded—in a brief, rapid rise—in bringing all Syria west of the Euphrates under its rule, until Roman attacks put an end to the kingdom of Palmyra.

Syrian polycentrism and particularism favoured the intervention of foreign powers which aimed at conquering it because of its position and wealth. Syria was again and again the target of foreign armies which often enough fought out their battles on its territory. After the middle of the 3rd millennium it was first the Mesopotamian kings of the Akkad dynasty who stretched out their hands to Syria and for a time brought parts of the country under their rule. Before the middle of the 2nd millennium, after a period in which a number of Syrian states flourished and showed signs of foreign influence only in the economic and cultural fields, the Hittites of Asia Minor appeared on the scene. They contended for control of Syria against Mitanni in Upper Mesopotamia and against Egypt, and finally succeeded in dominating the entire country as far as Homs and beyond in the south. At this time another power —Assyria—appeared on the eastern borders of Syria and its armies marched westward.

But first, about 1200 B.C., a re-grouping occurred which also changed the ethnic and political picture of Syria. During the period of migrations of maritime tribes, foreign tribes and peoples penetrated into Syrian territory and Aramaic tribes from the North Syrian steppes also exerted increasing pressure on the cultivated regions. A number of new kingdoms—headed partly by Aramaic, partly by Asia Minor dynasties—replaced Hittite and Egyptian domination of Syrian territory; these were the targets of Assyrian expansion in the subsequent period. Thus internal conflicts between the Syrian kingdoms and constant attacks by the Assyrians left their mark on Syrian political history during the first centuries of the 1st millennium B.C., the Early Iron Age. The Assyrians finally succeeded in incorporating Syria into their empire and dividing it up into a number of provinces. But they constantly had to fight new campaigns to maintain control of this valuable territory. When the Assyrian Empire collapsed towards the end of the 7th century B.C. under the combined attacks of the Medes of Iran and the Chaldaean Babylonians, the Neo Babylonian Kingdom of Nebuchadnezzar superseded it in Syria. Nebuchadnezzar succeeded in defeating the Egyptians, who had taken advantage of the situation to press forward to the north as far as the Euphrates. The Neo Babylonian rulers of Syria were followed by the Persians. After the middle of the 6th century B.C. Syria, in which local dynasties continued to exist, belonged to the Persian Empire and was one of its most important satrapies.

Alexander of Macedonia—later called "the Great"—entered Syria in 333 B.C. after the victorious battle of Issus. He passed through the country twice—once on his way to Egypt and again on his march to Mesopotamia into the heart of his Persian enemy's territory. When the conqueror died in Babylon in June 323 B.C. the struggle for his heritage broke

out among his generals. Seleucus succeeded in gaining control of Syria in 301 B.C. This was the beginning of two-and-a-half centuries of Seleucid rule. The capital was outside the frontiers of what is now the Syrian Arab Republic, at the mouth of the Orontes—Antioch (now Antakya). Syria became an integral part of the Greek world; here Orient and Occident touched and united culturally to a hitherto unknown extent and the big cities, especially the new cities founded by the Seleucids, were almost completely Hellenised. But outside the cities the old Orient lived on and lost little of its vitality. When the thin Greek upper layer cracked, the Oriental element took on new life everywhere.

The rule of the Seleucids, who had already lost the regions east of the Euphrates to the Parthians in the 2nd century B.C., was finally brought to an end by the Romans. In 64 B.C. Pompey appeared in Syria with an army and incorporated the country into the expanding Empire; Syria remained under its rule for several hundred years. In the 3rd century Palmyra was able to profit by its intermediate position between the Romans and the Sassanids of Persia, who replaced the Parthians in Mesopotamia. It became independent and extended its influence as far as Egypt, but collapsed in 273 and never again attained its former importance.

When the Roman Empire was divided into two parts in 395, Syria fell to the Eastern Roman Empire of Byzantium. The eastern Euphrates regions remained in the hands of the Sassanids. Only in the mid-7th century did the political situation change completely. Under the banner of the Prophet, the Arab Moslems also attacked Syria and conquered it within a few years. A new era—the Islamic

era—began, during which Syria rose to new heights, first as a centre and then as one of the provinces of the Caliphate.

THE INHABITANTS OF ANCIENT SYRIA

We do not know who were the earliest inhabitants of what is now the Syrian Arab Republic. We know neither what they looked like nor what they were called. The population of this territory certainly did not form an entity in very ancient times. It is probable that Semitic tribes soon joined the inhabitants, whom we can only describe as pre-Semitic and of whom we have only material evidence and none through inscriptions. At the time when Syria is first mentioned in written sources, that is, in the second half of the 3rd millennium, there was a numerous Semitic population, and towards the end of the 3rd millennium the politically dominant stratum in particular belonged to the West Semitic-Amorite section of the population. We find the same population element at this time in Mesopotamia and in Palestine, and we shall not be far wrong in seeking its origin in the North Syrian steppes. In the following period other Semitic tribes from the same area penetrated into the cultivated regions of Syria; in the cuneiform inscriptions they are called Sutaeans, Akhlamaeans or, towards the end of the 2nd millennium, Aramaeans. The last great immigration of Semitic tribal groups was that of the Arabs, whose presence can be shown in the first half of the 1st millennium B.C. They gained political power in various parts of Syria, in Hauran and Palmyra, for example, long before the Islamic conquerors brought a strongly Arab influence into the whole of Syria.

In addition to these inhabitants of Syria who belonged to the Semitic language group, immigrants from other regions should be mentioned: the Khurrites, for example, who came from the mountains of northeastern West Asia and appeared first in Upper Mesopotamia and then, after the early 2nd millennium, in Syria itself. They succeeded in gaining political control in some Syrian centres. About the middle of the 2nd millennium Indo-Aryan elements also advanced as far as Syria and in the Mitanni state in Upper Mesopotamia they attained a leading position. Towards the end of the 2nd millennium maritime tribes came from the Balkans, invaded West Asia and also passed through Syria. Since they were held up here by the Egyptians, some of them will have settled in Syria. Peoples from Asia Minor who were of Indo-Germanic origin were also driven southeast into Syria as a result of the migration of maritime tribes.

Apart from those who reached Syria as a result of migrations, other foreigners came and remained as traders, officials or soldiers, mixing with the indigenous population. It is certain, for example, that this was the case with immigrants from Egypt, from the Aegean and Asia Minor, from Assyria and Babylonia and from Persia and the Graeco-Roman Mediterranean world. Syria became a melting-pot of peoples and tribes out of which developed the population which we call Syrians; these re-shaped a variety of traditions and were amongst the economically and culturally most advanced peoples in the ancient world.

THE ANCIENT ORIENTAL PERIOD

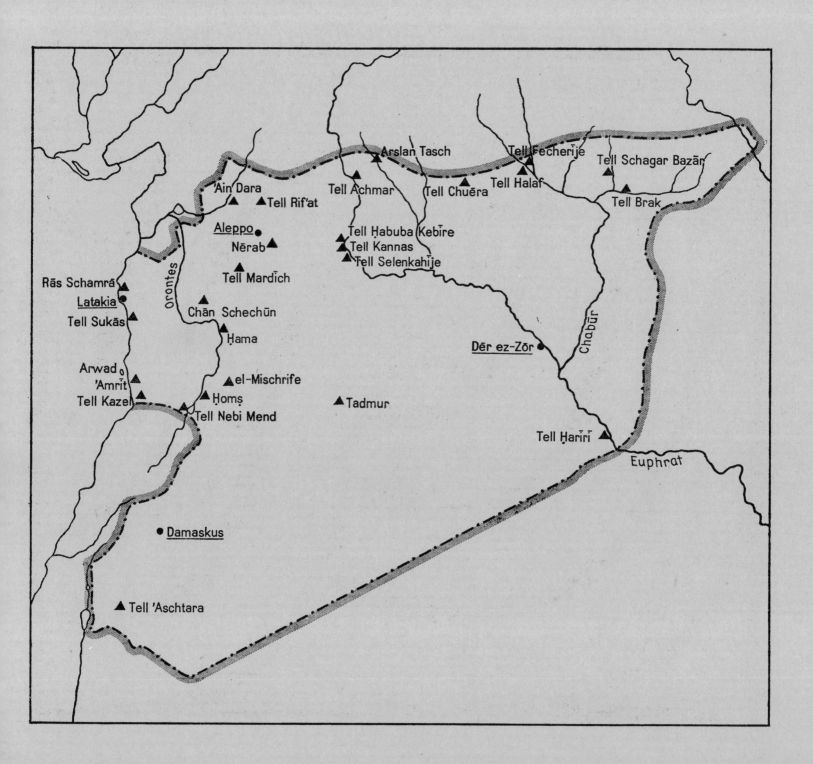

Arslan Tasch

Tell Fecherije

Tell Schagar Bazār

'Ain Dara

Tell Rif'at

Tell Achmar

Tell Chuēra

Tell Halaf

Tell Brak

Aleppo

Nērab

Tell Ḥabuba Kebīre

Tell Kannas

Tell Selenkahīje

Tell Mardīch

Rās Schamrā

Latakia

Tell Sukās

Orontes

Chān Schechūn

Ḥama

Dēr ez-Zōr

Chabūr

Arwad

'Amrīt

el-Mischrife

Tadmur

Tell Kazel

Ḥoms

Tell Nebi Mend

Tell Ḥarīrī

Euphrat

Damaskus

Tell 'Aschtara

The beehive shaped houses of this village are typical for northern Syria. It lies at the foot of a big tell, a mound of ruins which are the result of long years of settlement. French excavations conducted here show that settlement must have gone on for a long time.

MARI (TELL HARIRI). Clay model of a round house with several rooms grouped round a central courtyard (?). The model has a diameter of 54 cm and dates back to the middle of the 3rd millennium, the first golden age of Mari. Damascus, National Museum.

MARI. The buildings in this city were of mud bricks, as was usual in Mesopotamia. The clay plentiful in the Euphrates Valley was mixed with finely-chopped straw, pressed into bricks and then dried in the sun. The binding between the bricks in the wall can be seen clearly. The buildings excavated weather rapidly and collapse again.

MARI. In the area containing the great royal palace, which dates back to the early 2nd millennium B.C., deeper-going excavations have brought to light palace buildings of the early dynastic period (c. mid-3rd millennium). The picture shows excavations in the courtyard of the oldest early dynastic palace. A cesspool of Zimrilim's palace ran through this courtyard; it was built of ceramic rings each 55 cm in height and 95 cm in diameter.

MARI. *Early dynastic buildings near the temple tower (Ziggurat) of Mari. They were destroyed by fire. Behind the ruins the Euphrates Valley to whose fertile soil Mari owed its existence.*

MARI. *Statue of a goddess of water, white stone, height 1.42 m. The figure was found in the palace of King Zimrilim of Mari and dates back to about 1800 B.C. The goddess, whose eyes are inlaid, holds a vessel in her hand from which life-giving water flows. Wavy lines and fish are chiselled into the long, flowing robe symbolising over-flowing water. There is a channel inside the vessel through which water could be forced so that it actually overflowed and ran down the figure; this was certainly done during cultic ceremonies. Similar figures are often found in Mesopotamian art. Aleppo, Museum.*

MARI. *Painting from the great palace of King Zimrilim, c. 1800 B.C. The picture shows a section of a sacrificial procession. The hand covering part of the head belongs to a much larger figure leading the procession, probably the king or priest. Paris, Louvre.*

MARI. *Alabaster statue of Iku-Shamagan. The donor of this figure, which is 1.12 m in height, was a member of a Semitic dynasty and King of Mari about the middle of the 3rd millennium. The statue is especially remarkable because of the well-preserved head and expressive eyes, once inlaid in colour. It was found in 1952 during excavations in the Ninni-Zaza shrine at Mari. Damascus, National Museum.*

TELL MARDIKH. *South gate in the city wall (Sector A). In the foreground, remains of the orthostats forming the entrance. To the left, behind this, a part of the entrance court can be seen. The gate provided entry to the city from the south and was 21.5 m long and 5 m wide comprising two main rooms with double niches and an ante-room.*

TELL MARDIKH. *Eastern side of the second entry-way of the south gate. The orthostats—resting on stone pedestals—which covered the walls are especially well preserved here and form a niche. Behind this a wall overgrown with grass rises to the right, with the old city wall under this.*

TELL MARDIKH. *View from the south of the diggings in Sector B in the lower town. The square-hewn stones are part of the remains of store-rooms.*

TELL MARDIKH. *Diggings in Sector D of the western part of the acropolis. The remains of buildings with the bases of pillars belong to a sanctuary.*

TELL MARDIKH. *A royal palace was laid bare in the northern part of the acropolis during excavations in Sector E; here the northern courtyard and two rows of rooms can be seen. This highest point of Tell Mardikh offers a broad view over the lower town and the North Syrian plain.*

TELL MARDIKH. *In the foreground below are the remains of the southern entrance to the north courtyard of the palace which excavations in Sector E brought to light. Above this parts of the foundations of later buildings can be seen. In spring, as the photograph shows, this part is covered with tall grasses and some of it even sown to grain. Italian excavations always start after the harvest.*

UGARIT. *This ivory head, 15 cm in height, is one of the most beautiful single finds in Ugarit. It dates from the 2nd quarter of the 2nd millennium and obviously represents a juvenile god—perhaps Baal. The head was gilded, the eyes and eyebrows inlaid in colour. Damascus, National Museum.*

UGARIT. The fortress-like western extremity of the great royal palace, which reaches a height of not less than 6 m, has in it the entrance to a postern, an underground passage-way with bracket vaulting. In the event of attack, people could withdraw quickly from the harbour district inside the palace walls or sally out against besiegers through this passage-way. There is a curve in the passage, which reaches a height of up to 5 m. A flight of shallow steps leads up to the level of the royal palace. The entrance is hidden by a tower. The block which served as a lintel is 2 m wide.

UGARIT. From the postern gate one enters a fore-court and the guard-room beside the entrance to the great palace. The stones used to close the three-cornered peep-holes can be pushed out from inside but cannot be removed from the outside. The way up to the palace could be kept well in view through the peep-holes.

UGARIT. Shallow steps lead from outside into the palace forecourt. The picture shows one of the two stone bases at the entrance on which stood the wooden pillars supporting the lintel. Behind the walls which can be seen in the background are a number of smaller rooms called the "western archives" because of the documents discovered in them.

UGARIT. *The great palace courtyard I is paved and contains a fountain with a monolithic framework; it still gives potable water. Behind it there is a water-trough with a gutter.*

UGARIT. *The paving of the great courtyard is well preserved. This courtyard can be entered through the northern gate on the way from the postern and the guardroom farther into the grounds of the great palace.*

UGARIT. *In courtyard II of the great royal palace a brazier and the remains of stairs were found.*

UGARIT. *Like the residential district, the royal palace had a drainage system and a number of water-pipes and basins.*

UGARIT. *The outer wall of the great palace, with its well-hewn square stones, is especially well preserved on the side opposite to the small palace.*

UGARIT. *There was also a necropolis in the great palace. Steps led down into the underground burial chambers in which members of the royal family were interred.*

UGARIT. *The most important sacred place of Ugarit was probably the temple of the weather god Baal, the "ruler". Little remains of the temple itself. In the foreground, the altar in front of the cella.*

UGARIT. *Two gold bowls decorated with relief lines were found near the temple of Baal. The diameter of the bowl shown here is 18.5 cm. Inside on the bottom there are two rows of figures, the upper row depicting a hunting scene and the lower row goats running. Aleppo, Museum.*

UGARIT. *The southern residential district of the city shows a confusion of lanes and houses where bustling oriental life once prevailed. A private scientific library was also found in this district.*

UGARIT. *This view of the southeast district of the city, which shows only a small part of the area so far excavated on Ras Shamra, gives some idea not only of the size and importance of this Syrian harbour city, but also of the work done by French archaeologists and Syrian workers under the guidance of Cl. F.-A. Schaeffer.*

TIL BARSIP (TELL AKHMAR). *The weather god was especially revered throughout that part of Syria where agriculture was based on rainfall and numerous statues and reliefs depicting this fertility-giving god have been discovered. A stele came to light in Tell Akhmar on the Euphrates during French excavations which shows the weather god in relief on its front side; he stands on the* sacred bull, *holding in his hands a double-headed axe and a bundle of lightning. The horned hat indicates the godly nature of the figure. Above the weather god, a winged solar disk—a symbol widespread also in West Asia. The stele, which probably dates from the 11th century B.C., has an inscription on three sides in the so-called Hittite hieroglyphic script. Aleppo, Museum.*

TIL BARSIP. *Wall painting from the palace of the Assyrian governor; section (height 40.7 cm). It probably dates from the reign of the Assyrian King Tiglath-pileser III (745–727) and depicts two dignitaries. Aleppo, Museum.*

TELL KAZEL. *Syrian excavations at this tell near the Mediterranean coast, which may be old Simyra—brought to light local and impordet ceramics. The photograph shows an example of local ware of the Late Bronze Age, discovered in Stratum V. Damascus, National Museum.*

KHADATU (ARSLAN TASH). *We owe a number of ivory plates from the bed of King Hazael of Damascus to the work of French archaeologists; these were made in the 9th century B.C. An ivory plate nearly 20 cm in length is reproduced here; it shows two winged rams wearing the Egyptian double crown and is part of a panel which is slightly curved to accord with its use. The rams are given the bodies of lions. The stylised tree between the two legendary animals probably represents the sacred date palm. Aleppo, Museum.*

GUZANA (TELL HALAF). *This basalt relief—1.4 m in width and 1.25 m in height—was found during German excavations at Tell Halaf in the far north of what is now the Syrian Arab Republic. Two bull-men hold aloft a winged solar disk; they stand on a stool-like pediment. In the centre, a kneeling man supports the arms of the two creatures. The eyes of the two creatures and the solar disk were inlaid. The relief dates back to the 8th century B.C. Aleppo, Museum.*

MARATHUS ('AMRIT). "El-Ma-abed" (the temple) is the name given by the Arabs of this area to the sanctuary laid bare by the Syrian Ancient Monuments Administration. The sanctum rises up out of the centre of a sacred pool fed from a spring flowing out of a grotto. It stands on a high base chiselled out of the rock, opens to the north and has two crowns of pinnacles. This structure dates from about the 5th to 4th century B.C. and bears clearly oriental features.

MARATHUS. The sacred pool of the "Water Temple" was surrounded by a pathway 5 m wide, which was paved and had a portico, some of whose monolithic pillars, of a height up to 3 m, still remain. The depth of the shrine which was hewn out of the rock can be clearly seen. The depth of the pool itself—now almost filled up with fallen stones—was a further three metres.

MARATHUS. *The northern "spindle", with one of the four lions which rise above the base and were also intended to protect the monument.*

MARATHUS. *These burial monuments—"spindles"—can be seen from afar. The base of the monument in front is decorated with the fore-quarters of four lions, the round upper part with two rows of toothed markings ends in a half-globe. The other monument ends in a pentagonal pyramid at the top.*

MARATHUS. *The burial towers, called "spindles" by the local population, which probably date from the 2nd or 1st century B.C., are landmarks of the old Marathus which can be seen from afar. These are massive monuments whose burial chambers can be reached from outside by a passage.*

MARATHUS. *Amongst the small finds in 'Amrit special attention should be directed to the head of a stone statuette which combines Oriental and Graeco-Arab features and perhaps dates back to the 5th to 4th centuries B.C. Damascus, National Museum.*

MARATHUS. *The southern burial-monument, rising from a low, two-step pedestal.*

MARATHUS. *A narrow passage leads to the burial chambers underneath the monument—here the south monument. The entrance was closed by stone blocks.*

The transition from hunting and gathering food to settled arable farming took place very early in Syria, before the 7th millennium. Excavations such as those conducted at Ras Shamra and Tell Sukas on the Syrian coast, in Hama on the middle reaches of the Orontes and at Tell Ramad near Qatana in southern Syria, which are still going on, make it possible to follow cultural developments in the region of what is now the Syrian Arab Republic since Neolithic times. Towards the end of the 5th millennium the use of metal —copper—increased to such an extent that we can speak of a Copper-Stone Age from that time on; about a millennium later, around 3000 B.C., began the Bronze Age. Archaeological discoveries show clearly how town settlements developed in this long pre-historic period, division of labour within society increased and social differentiations emerged more and more clearly. Syria was mentioned for the first time in Mesopotamian and Egyptian inscriptions in the 3rd millennium—in the Early Bronze Age. These sources show that in the most advanced regions of Syria states were formed in which those in control sought to establish their power and wealth at the expense of other strata of the population—states, with a class society whose first stage of development we shall here call the ancient oriental period.

Roughly speaking, this period covers two millennia. Although there are still big gaps in the evidence, both from the point of view of space and time, it is possible to follow the developments which took place in Syria during this period at least in outline. We owe this especially to extensive archaeological research and to the efforts of historians and philologists who opened up the evidence of inscriptions and interpreted it. In regard to ancient oriental ruins, Syrian archaeology is relatively young. Since only a few excavation sites can be shown here pictorially, the most important research work must at least be noted briefly.

A German expedition under Freiherr von Oppenheim began work at Tell Halaf in Upper Mesopotamia, now close to the Turkish frontier, in 1911; this was resumed in 1927. In addition to pre-historic finds of great importance, an Aramaic royal residence of the Early Iron Age was exposed here whose statues and orthostat reliefs provide adequate evidence of the art of the early 1st millennium B.C. French excavations at Tell Nebi Mend, about 20 km south of Homs, began in 1921. They were directed by M. Pézard and laid free the old city of Kadesh which is often mentioned in inscriptions of the 2nd millennium; the famous battle between the Hittites and the troops of Rameses II of Egypt was fought near here. The big Tell el-Mishrife lies northeast of Homs, in the fertile Central Syrian plains. Investigations began here in 1924, under R. du Mesnil du Buisson, which throw some light on the lay-out of the town of Qatna, mentioned in texts of the 2nd millennium. Tell Rif'at, 35 km northwest of Haleb-Aleppo, was the destination of a Czech expedition in 1924; the royal Aramaic residence of Arpad was re-discovered in this great tell. As the excavations continued by English archaeologists in 1960 show, this place was already inhabited in the Copper-Stone Age. French researchers succeeded in 1926–1927 in rescuing a number of cuneiform tablets of the 6th century B.C. on the Nerab site somewhat southeast of Aleppo. The ivory carvings discovered during French excava-tions at Arslan Tash near the Turkish frontier are now famous; they date back to the 8th century B.C. and were found in a building near the palace of the Assyrian king Tiglath-Pileser III (745–727). The city whose lay-out French archaeologists headed by F. Thureau-Dangin, were able to clarify in 1927–1929, was called Khadatu. Not far from Arslan Tash lies Tell Akhmar, on the eastern bank of the Euphrates, the site of the ancient Til Barsip. Archaeological work was done here by Thureau-Dangin and M. Dunand after 1929 and was crowned by the discovery of magnificent wall-paintings in the palace of the Assyrian governor. In the same year excavations began in Ras Shamra which, along with those in Mari, may be regarded as the most important ancient oriental excavations in the territory of the Syrian Arab Republic. Both these sites will be described in more detail. R. du Mesnil du Buisson, who has worked in many places in Syria and is at present investigating Bronze Age Palmyra, undertook excavations at the great Tell Khan Shekhun in Central Syria in 1930; there is evidence that this place was a settlement for a long period of time. The Central and northern Syrian plains, which are rich in tells—one can sometimes see several at the same time—will certainly yield many more discoveries in the future.

A tell in the middle of the town of Hama which, with its great water wheels on the Orontes and its numerous fine Arab houses, is certainly one of the most interesting and picturesque Syrian towns, was investigated after 1931 by a Danish team under H. Ingholt. Excavations done here show that it was already a settlement in the Neolithic Age. Hama-Hamath played a role as an important

Aramaic state in the early 1st millennium B.C.

Three other ruined sites in the northeastern part of the Syrian Arab Republic deserve mention here. As is the case with others in this region, they owed their settlement to the higher rainfall which permitted permanent arable farming. Of these Tell Shagar Bazar deserves to be mentioned first; its history can be traced back to the 2nd millennium B.C. as a result of important single finds by the English expedition under M. E. L. Mallowan in 1935–1936. Excavations by another expedition under Mallowan, at Tell Brak, produced interesting results including a temple of the early 3rd millennium and a palace of the time of the Kings of Akkad (24th to 22nd centuries). Finally, mention should be made of the American research work done at Tell Fekherije on the Upper Khabur in 1940, which was continued by a West German expedition under A. Moortgat in 1955–1956. This great tell, which had already been surveyed by M. von Oppenheim, contained remains of a settlement dating mainly from the middle of the 2nd millennium, the Khurrite Mitannic period. But it has so far not been possible to establish definitely whether, as is assumed, the capital of Mitanni stood here.

As this brief survey of excavations up to the outbreak of World War II shows, archaeological investigations in Syria increased in extent during this period. French scholars have an especially big share in them. After the country was separated from the Osman Turkish Empire which collapsed during World War I, it came under French mandate. In 1941 Syria became an independent Republic and in April 1946 the last French troops left the country. The investigations of ancient oriental ruins have been conducted to an increasing extent by the Syrians themselves.

Syrian excavations under F. Serafi began in 'Ain Dara, northwest of Aleppo, in 1956. Layers of settlements from the first half of the 1st millennium B.C. were laid bare and a number of orthostat reliefs and figures of lions discovered. In the same year the Ancient Monuments Administration of the Syrian Arab Republic began investigating Tell Kazel (Page 42), which lies on the Lebanese frontier near the coast; the work was directed by M. Dunand, A. Bounni and N. Saliby, and continued the search for the old Sumur-Simyra so often mentioned in the sources. This search was begun before World War II by R. Braidwood at the nearby Tell Simirijan. It has so far not been possible to equate Tell Kazel definitely with old Sumur, but the archaeological finds dating from the Late Bronze and Early Iron Age would indicate this. Tell Sukas, south of Latakia, which has already been mentioned, is also on the coast. Here a Danish research team headed by P. J. Riis has since 1958 made a valuable contribution to Syrian pre-historic research and has also excavated material from the Bronze and Iron Ages. This site can probably be identified as Shuksi, a place mentioned in Ugarit texts. Somewhat south of Tartus, opposite the island of Ruad (Arwad), lie the widespread ruins of 'Amrit. Although most of the ancient monuments discovered here are of ancient Greek origin, some of the buildings—for instance the water shrine investigated by the Ancient Monuments Administration—may date back to ancient oriental times. 'Amrit will therefore be presented in this book as an example of the architecture of the period of transition to Hellenism.

The West German excavations at Tell Khuera under A. Moortgat, which began in 1958, again bring us to the northeast of the Syrian Arab Republic. Here remains of buildings of the 3rd millennium and some praying figures are amongst the finds of greatest cultural and historical importance. On the Hauran plain south of Damascus, at the other end of the Republic, Tell 'Ashtara—the Ashtaroth of the Bible—was investigated by A. Abu Assaf, who was able to determine that there had been a Bronze Age settlement here. The building of the Euphrates dam, which will lead to the flooding of a large section of the Euphrates valley near Meskene, has also led to a number of archaeological investigations. Of the excavations begun here, which have started very promisingly and have also produced material for the ancient oriental period, only Tell Selenkahije, Tell Kannas and Tell Habuba Kebire, where American, Belgian and West German expeditions are at work, will be mentioned here.

It would take us too far to note all the prospecting, surface diggings and smaller excavations which have broadened our knowledge of the ancient oriental history of Syria. A number of important and informative single discoveries were made in places where no research work had so far been done, and in other places—in Damascus and Aleppo, the two biggest cities in the Syrian Arab Republic, for example—new buildings have prevented more extensive archaeological investigations. That the number of settlements in Syria during the ancient oriental period was very considerable is shown especially by the many place names to be found in the written sources, although it must be assumed that the majority of these consisted of only a few buildings. Syrian archaeology is only on the threshold of promising discoveries, notwithstanding more than fifty years of successful work.

Most of the numerous finds dating from ancient oriental times are today in museums. What is left on the excavation sites, especially the remains of excavated buildings, is generally not worth visiting, for there is little left to see after excavations have been completed and climatic influences have done their work of destruction over a period of years. Anyone whose idea of ruined sites is based on Pompeii, Baalbek or Palmyra may well be disappointed by a visit to most of the sites of ancient oriental excavations. This applies especially to the Mesopotamian part of the Syrian Arab Republic, where the walls were almost all of mud bricks. All stone reliefs and statues discovered were placed in museums and rain, wind and sun have destroyed more and more of what remained. But the importance of these sites is not to be measured so much by what remains to be seen there or what found a place in museums; much more important is what scientists have been able to interpret from the archaeological finds. An apparently modest pottery vessel, a small statuette or the meagre remains of a building can sometimes be as exciting and interesting to the expert as an example of ancient temple architecture still standing. In looking at the illustrations on the following pages, therefore, one should bear in mind the cultural and material achievements once attained on these sites—achievements like script and letters drawn on tablets of damp clay and conserved down to our own day

by means of drying or burning, invaluable sources of knowledge about daily life in early Syria, of information about religion and literature, the beginnings of the natural sciences and political history. It is certainly no accident that script was first developed into an alphabet in Syria, where the most varied influences from the highly developed cultures of the Euphrates and the Nile converged. Mari and Ugarit are amongst the ruined sites in the Near East which have contributed most to expanding our knowledge of ancient West Asia, because of the discovery of numerous inscriptions made there.

MARI (TELL HARIRI)

We owe to an accident one of the most important discoveries of our century in oriental archaeology. In August 1933 Bedouins camping on the middle reaches of the Orontes buried a member of their tribe at Tell Hariri, 11 km northwest of Abu Kemal. Searching for a large stone to protect the corpse from wild animals, they came upon the statue of a bearded man. One of the Bedouins reported the find to a French officer, Lieutenant Cabane, on duty in Abu Kemal. He had the 300 kg statue dug up and brought to Abu Kemal and reported to the office responsible, at that time the Ancient Monuments Administration in Beirut, which then sent an official to bring the statue to the Museum of Aleppo. In October 1933 it was decided in Paris to conduct excavations at Tell Hariri. A. Parrot was entrusted with this work, which began on December 14th that year and has continued—in one expedition each year—from 1933 to 1939, from 1951 to 1955 and again since 1961.

Some statues were dug up in 1934 of which three had inscriptions on the right shoulder. One of these reads: "Lamgi-Mari, King of Mari, High Priest of the God Enlil, has dedicated his statue to the Goddess Ishtar". Thus Tell Hariri harbours the remains of the old city of Mari, whose name was already known from cuneiform texts. The identification by the American archaeologist W. F. Albright in 1926 was thus confirmed.

The excavations here enable us to trace the development of Mari far back into the 3rd millennium, into the so-called early dynastic period of Mesopotamia. Some sanctuaries at Mari were founded in that period and the most recent excavations in the region of the great royal palace (Page 17) show that a number of palaces were built on the same site one after another from the early dynastic period onwards. There were numerous finds at Mari, including praying figures with folded hands set up, as permanent monuments of their donors, facing the pictures of the gods in the temples (Page 23). The names of persons given in the inscriptions clearly show that Mari was at that time the residence of a Semitic dynasty; in the following period, too, an important route used by nomad Semitic tribes immigrating into civilised Mesopotamia ran close by Mari.

We learn nothing from the dedication inscriptions on the statues about the role which Mari played in the early dynastic period, but from other sources we know that this flourishing and favourably situated city attracted the troops of foreign princes. It may be that the destruction of an early dynastic palace at Mari indicated by archaeological discoveries can be linked up with military events connected with the advance of King Sargos of

53

Akkad (c. 2300) *(Page 20)*. The South Mesopotamian kings of Ur later spread their rule as far as the middle Euphrates and had Mari administered by governors. But at that time Semitic nomads—the Amorites—began to penetrate in increasing numbers into Mesopotamia and some smaller states developed on the ruins of the Kingdom of Ur; these included the rising Kingdoms of Assur on the Tigris and Babylon on the Euphrates and also Mari.

After the pre-Sargonic period Mari experienced a second great golden age, and French excavations have produced impressive evidence of this. Historically, the excavation of the royal archives of Mari, in which thousands of clay tablets with cuneiform inscriptions were found, was certainly the most important discovery; so far about 25,000 clay tablets have come to light. The texts—in Babylonian—include letters, documents connected with economy and administration and inscriptions of a religious character. This extensive material also throws light on the situation in civilised Syria west of the desert, which was at that time divided up into a number of kingdoms and tribal territories.

The last king to reign in Mari was called Zimrilim; his rule came to a violent end before the middle of the 18th century B.C. The palace in which he and his predecessors had resided has been excavated by the French expedition over a period of years. It is one of the biggest palace sites of the old Near East; on an area of about nine acres there are more than three hundred rooms and courtyards, a conglomeration of many dwelling-houses clustered together, several rooms opening on to a courtyard and getting their light from it *(Page 55)*. The mud-brick walls of the palace *(Page 17)* were carefully dug out by the excavators and still stand to a height of five metres, so that one can again wander through the rooms of the old royal residence (where this is not prevented by current excavations which go deeper). The great throne room, 26 metres long, was at the centre of this profusion of rooms, courtyards and passages and the ruler's canopied throne stood on a platform here. The royal apartments and the houses of the courtiers, workshops and storerooms, kitchens and bathrooms with pottery bathtubs, a palace school with clay seats, and various offices, were also to be found within the palace walls. A great number of important monuments, including the famous statue of a goddess of rain *(Page 21)*, were excavated in the royal palace. The wall-paintings found in various rooms are especially interesting *(Page 22)*; these depict mainly cultic or religious themes.

In addition to the great palace, which was already famous in its own day, and some residential areas, a number of sanctuaries were excavated in Mari. A massive temple tower, built of mud bricks, already dominated the city in its early golden age in the 3rd millennium.

Inscriptions tell us little about the end of the metropolis on the Euphrates which can be so clearly interpreted from the archaeological discoveries. Brief notices from Babylonian South Mesopotamia indicate that King Hammurabi of Babylon attacked his erstwhile ally Zimrilim of Mari and captured his residence. When an uprising against the Babylonian occupation broke out the city was destroyed—an event which may well have taken place about 1760 B.C. Mari never recovered from this blow. Some centuries

MARI. *Palace of King Zimrilim, c. 1800 B.C. Perspective reconstruction. After A. Parrot, Sumer (Munich 1960), Plate 321.*

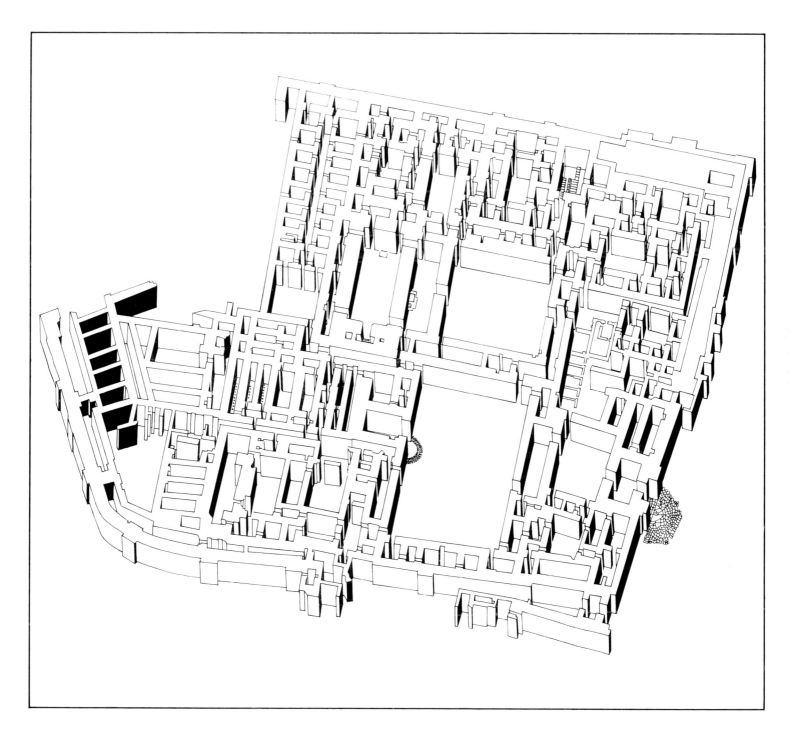

55

later there were only a few poor houses amongst the ruins of the former metropolis, and the Assyrians stationed a garrison here. For many centuries Mari was no more than a cemetery, shored up by sand and washed over by rain, until a burial occasioned its re-discovery.

Tell Mardikh

The site now to be described cannot compare in importance with Mari or Ugarit. Nevertheless, it is included here, firstly, to draw the observer's attention to the numerous tells of the central and northern Syrian plains as well as to those on the Euphrates (Mari), and on the Mediterranean (Ugarit, Marathos), and secondly, as an example of excavations begun recently and showing promise, but in which the area of one-time settlement has not yet been fully exposed. Much can therefore still be expected; we shall certainly gain more exact knowledge in the near future about the settlement which once covered this site.

Tell Mardikh lies about 70 km south of Aleppo. The asphalt road connecting Damascus via Homs and Hama with central North Syria passes close by it. An archaeological expedition of the University of Rome, headed by P. Matthiae, conducted investigations in this region in 1964. Tell Mardikh was selected as the excavation site; it is near the village of the same name, with its beehive shaped houses which are typical for northern Syria. The outline of the site shows that it consisted of an acropolis, a lower town and a circular wall surrounding both. This form distinguishes Tell Mardikh from most of the other tells in the region, which are generally broad mounds flattened at the top. This gave rise to the assumption that an old royal residence might be found at Tell Mardikh. The ruins cover an area of about 900 m by 700 m, almost oval in shape. The highest point is 13 m above the surrounding country.

The Italian excavations have so far been conducted in five different places and it has been possible, mainly on the evidence of pottery finds, to date most of the remains where work has begun back to the Middle Bronze Age (2100–1600). At that time there was a ruler's residence here and the town was probably called Ebla, a name often mentioned in cuneiform texts. Up to the present, the south city gate, two temples, a palace and a number of dwellinghouses have been excavated. The big city gate, partly built of well-hewn stone blocks, which was discovered in Sector A of the excavations (Pages 24, 57) is impressive. In Sector B, in the lower town, a Middle Bronze Age temple and a settlement strata (Page 25) were found. Digging is in progress in two sectors on the acropolis; in Sector D a big temple emerged (Page 25) which measures 18.5 m by 11.2 m and was divided into three rooms of equal breadth. The entrance was from the south and the cultic niche was on the north wall. This building, too, probably dates from the Middle Bronze Age, like the south gate and the temple in the lower town. The most important discovery yet made here is probably the big limestone basin (Pages 26, 27) which is decorated with reliefs on three sides. A similar fragment in the Aleppo museum, which also comes from Tell Mardikh, and fragments of other basins, indicate that such containers, obviously intended to hold water, played a role in the cult of this city. In another sector of the excavations on the acropolis (E) five layers of settlement were laid bare and also a palace. On this evidence the ruler's residence was situated at the highest point of the city (Pages 28, 57).

Diggings at Tell Mardikh are only beginning, but the work done so far indicates that much can still be expected.

Ugarit (Ras Shamra)

Unlike Tell Mardikh, the site of one-time Ugarit has been the scene of a considerable number of excavations which have changed and enriched the picture of Bronze Age Syria more than almost any other investigations. The discovery of this important site is also the result of an accident. In 1928 a peasant ploughing his field about 11 km north of Latakia came upon large, regularly hewn rocks. Further investigations revealed that they had been the roof of a grave. The French mandatory authorities took charge of the matter and an expedition began to investigate the site in 1929. It turned out that the harbour district of the town of Ugarit had been here, at the place now called Minet el-Beda. Excavations in Ugarit under Cl. F.-A. Schaeffer have continued since then—except during the war years. They will also yield interesting results in the years to come.

From the harbour district excavations were soon extended to the centre, on the neighbouring Ras Shamra, a mound over-grown with fennel. Deep diggings here revealed that Ugarit was settled by man as early as the 7th millennium, in the Later Stone Age; a wall about 5 m thick had protected it against attack. At the end of the 3rd millennium the settlement came to an abrupt end, as the ex-

TELL MARDIKH. *Sketch of the tell with surrounding wall and acropolis and the separate sectors of archaeological investigation (as of 1965). After Università degli Studi di Roma, Missione archeologica Italiana in Siria, Rapporto preliminare della Campagna 1965 (Tell Mardikh), Roma 1966, Vol. 1.*

1 = Section A
2 = Section B
3 = Section C
4 = Section D
5 = Section E

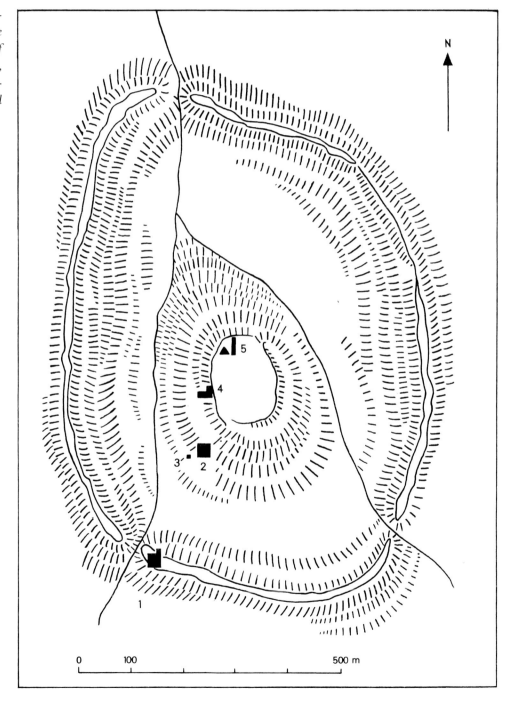

57

cavations show, and we may perhaps connect this with the immigration of a new population element, the West Semitic Amorites—something which can be shown to have occurred in a similar way in other parts of Syria. We meet the Amorites as the politically predominant element in the following period, as is also the case in Mari. The numerous texts of the 14th and 13th centuries discovered in Ugarit confirm that the ruling circles here were West Semitic Amorites.

The extremely successful archaeological research work done by Cl.F.-A.Schaeffer shows clearly that Ugarit reached its *floruit* during the Middle and Late Bronze Age (2100 to 1200). A catastrophe then occurred which completely destroyed it. The coastal region of Syria was again and again rocked by disastrous earthquakes and it would seem that Ugarit also suffered from such an earthquake shortly after 1200 B.C., as a result of which fire broke out. The town was abandoned by its inhabitants—insofar as they were able to escape—and never again settled. Earth piled up over the ruins and grass and weeds grew where there had once been the bustle of a wealthy trading city.

Its situation on a bay suitable for a harbour and a relatively broad and fertile hinterland gave Ugarit its importance and prosperity. Cyprus, called Alashiya in old texts, lies opposite to Ugarit; it was a natural station in trade between the Levant and the Aegean Sea. On the other hand the coastal mountains east of Ugarit were not high enough to hinder traffic into the Syrian hinterland and beyond to Mesopotamia. Thus the city was able to occupy an important place in trade during the Bronze Age; excavations have produced ample evidence of this. Products

UGARIT. *Burial place with a square-stone ceiling tapering to a sharp point and niches. After Cl.F.-A.Schaeffer, Ugaritica 1 (Paris 1939), Plate XVII, 1.*

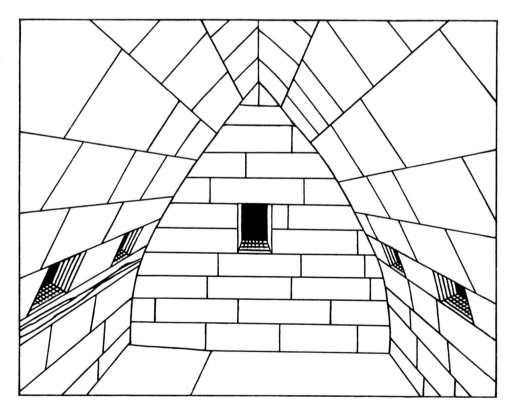

of the Aegean world, of Egypt and the West Asian hinterland became known to Ugarit, and foreign civilisation came to Ugarit along with the merchants, where it remained and mingled with other traditions. The Semitic (Canaanite) dynasty, which ruled in Ugarit from the early 2nd millennium, preferred "the Egyptian way of life", as the finds in the palace clearly show. And when Ugarit lost its political independence to the Hittites (mid-14th century B.C.) this strong Egyptian cultural influence brought in and carried on as a result of trading contacts also retained its importance in the North Syrian harbour city; being especially evident in court art.

French excavations have brought two palaces to light at Ras Shamra. The larger of these covers an area of about 9000 square metres and includes a number of courtyards and about sixty rooms (Pages 18, 30–34). Steps—of which there are some remains (Page 33)—led to the upper storey in which were the royal apartments and the audience hall (Page 34), and to the west an underground passage—a postern (Page 30)—enabled people to enter or leave the palace secretly. Houses of officials, merchants, craftsmen and priests were found in the residential part. Near the harbour there were not only store-rooms and merchants' offices; foreign merchants remaining for longer periods of time also lived here in a special district with their families. A large number of vaults built of square hewn stone were found in the harbour district, in the large and in the small palace, in the residential areas (Pages 34, 39, 58) and by the temples; those in the temples of Baal (Pages 36) and of Dagan deserve special mention. Their form recalls the graves of Mycenae.

Like the architecture, single discoveries also reflect the influence of eastern Mediterranean culture. Amongst the ceramics (Page 19) there are numerous vessels of the Minoan and Mycenaean type and an ivory carving of a goddess of fertility in Cretan dress standing between two goats. The influence of the Aegean can be seen in two gold bowls (Page 37) with reliefs of hunting scenes and other representations. Egyptian style can be clearly traced in the statuettes of deities (Page 29) which were found in large numbers, and in the ivory reliefs decorating the ruler's state bed. The native West Semitic culture of Ugarit can also be seen in many monuments found; it was often synthesised with the influences brought in from outside.

Inscriptions give the same picture; they lend even more importance to the excavations at Ugarit than the architecture or the single finds. Both in the various archives of the large royal palace and in the private collections of tablets, thousands of texts were discovered which tell us about the political life of the city, its economy and inhabitants, its literature and gods during the Later Bronze Age. Many of them are in Babylonian syllabic cuneiform script, the "diplomatic language" of the time. They deal mainly with Ugarit's relations to other kingdoms and especially to the Great Kings of the Hittites and their Syrian deputies, the viceroys of Karkemish (today Dyerabis on the Euphrates). Some of the tablets even come direct from the Hittite capital, Khattusha (today Boghazköy), brought there by messengers; after they had been dealt with they were placed in the archives.

In addition to some texts in the Khurrite language—mostly of a scholarly nature—and a few tablets with Cypriot-Minoan script,

thousands of documents were discovered at Ugarit which were in a script and language unknown until it was rediscovered. This turned out to be an alphabetic script using cuneiform characters—the first alphabet so far known to us. Both economic documents and literary writings were preserved in this script with 30 characters and in the West Semitic Ugarite language. In the literature in particular there are definite links with Mesopotamia on the one hand and with Aegaea on the other; parallels and conformities can also be found to the books of the Old Testament, but these owe their beginnings to a considerably later period.

In Ugarit's world of gods Baal, the god of rain and storms, takes first place. A number of legends exists about him, like that about the construction of his palace on Mount Zaphon, north of Ugarit, the present-day Djebel el-Akra. This mountain, rising almost 1800 m directly out of the ocean, whose peak was often veiled in clouds, seemed a suitable residence for Baal, rider of the clouds and god of thunder, who succeeded the old god of creation, El, as ruler of the world. The Ugarites' idea of gods differed greatly from that of the Mesopotamians which we can also see in Mari. On the other hand, there are obvious similarities with the ideas of the Greeks about the gods of Olympus.

The great variety in culture on Syrian soil can thus be very clearly seen in Ugarit, both in the archaeological findings and in the written sources.

Marathus ('Amrit)

When we leave Ugarit and visit 'Amrit in the southern part of the coastal region, we over-leap several hundred years. Thanks to the archaeological activities summarised above, we have a vast number of single finds, but there is no ruined site here which would give an adequate pictorial impression. Some single finds from Tell Halaf, Tell Akhmar and Arslan Tash are shown here (Pages 40–43) as examples of the art of this period, which was mainly shaped by the immigrant Aramaeans. These date from the early 1st millennium, when Aramaic and "neo-Hittite" kingdoms (founded by immigrant Luvians from Asia Minor) existed in the interior of Syria and the Phoenician trading cities on the coast of Lebanon spread their influence across the Mediterranean. There was certainly a settlement at that time where the ruins of 'Amrit now lie.

'Amrit, called Marathos in Greek inscriptions, lies a few kilometres south of Tartus; Tartus is the Antaradus of antiquity and the Tortosa of crusading times which is now gaining in importance for the Syrian Arab Republic as a harbour. Like Antaradus, Marathus was founded from the island of Aradus (today Ruad), which is about 4 km away from it. Its foundation probably had something to do with supplying the island city with food, drinking water and firewood. As a harbour Marathus can hardly have been important, although smaller ships could anchor at the mouth of the Nahr 'Amrit.

As the small number of inscriptions at Marathus indicate, the place belonged to the King of Aradus at the time of Alexander the Great. No further information is available at

UGARIT. *Alphabet Chart, pottery, found in the west archive of the city; c. 14th century B.C. It contains the characters of the Ugarit cuneiform alphabet. After a photo in the National Museum in Damascus.*

present and for the subsequent period the sources present no comprehensive picture of the historical development or role of Marathus. Since it is said to have been a "large and prosperous city" at the time of Alexander's campaign, it had probably existed for some time and grown up in the ancient oriental period. Incidental information provided by ancient writers, and the fact that the minting of coins in Marathus can be followed through three centuries, provides sparse evidence of the city's later existence; news of it ceases altogether after the time of the Roman Emperor Hadrian (117–138). Marathus' golden age was in Seleucid times and in the preceding period of Persian rule and the monuments which a visitor to 'Amrit sees today derive mainly from this period. But dates cannot always be definitely fixed here. The ruins which stood above-ground were investigated and sketched by E.Renan in 1860 and excavations by M.Dunand in 1926 and later work done by the Syrian Ancient Monuments Administration have considerably broadened this picture.

Syrian investigations were mainly concentrated on the sacred spring, called "el Ma'abed" (temple), which may date back to the turn of the 5th and 4th centuries B.C. *(Page 44)*. From 1957 to 1960 M.Dunand and N.Saliby undertook archaeological research here on behalf of the Directorate-General for Ancient Monuments and Museums of the Syrian Arab Republic which clarified the position with regard to the entire site of the sacred spring. This is a sacred pool measuring 38 by 48 m, hewn to a depth of 3 m out of the rock *(Page 45)*. It is surrounded by a path with porticoes some of whose monolithic pillars still stand to a height of 3 m. The pool is fed by a spring which emerges from a grotto on the southeast side and obviously played an important part in the cult. On a square underconstruction in the middle of the pool which was hewn out of the rock to its entire height of five-and-a-half metres stands the cella of the sanctuary. Closed in on three sides, it is crowned by a circle of pinnacles, above which there is another square structure, again crowned with pinnacles. In front of the cella, on the north side of the path, there was an altar on a small structure built into the pool, only the foundations of which remain today. Near the altar some small stone altars and stelae were discovered. On the north side of that path, here level with the sloping ground, there is a wall in which the entrance was to be found.

To the east of these very important remains of old Marathus, excavations have laid bare the ruins of dwellings which probably date back to the end of Persian rule over 'Amrit. Under these, Cypriot ceramics of the 6th century B.C. were found. To the north-east it is still possible to recognise seats of a stadium which attained its most recent form under the Romans but very probably dates back to the Hellenic period.

Among some other noteworthy buildings, some of which were also hewn out of the rocks and the remains of which—washed out by rain and often taking on bizarre shapes—are now favourite hiding-places for snakes, there are the three "spindles" (Arabic "maghazil"), remains of old Marathus which can be seen from afar *(Pages 46–48)*. These are burial monuments which were probably set up only in the 2nd or 1st century B.C. Two of them are only 6 metres apart, while the third stands a short distance away to the south *(Page 50)*. Passages lead from outside to the burial chambers under the "spindles" *(Page 50)*.

The remains of Marathus, which also include a stele now exhibited in the Louvre in Paris, are spread over a broad area, part of which is now farming land. Only a few of the monuments offer an impressive sight to the visitor, but the view over the Mediterranean to the island of Ruad will compensate even those who expected to find more here; this is especially true in spring, when the entire area is carpeted with gaily coloured flowers.

THE GRAECO-ROMAN PERIOD

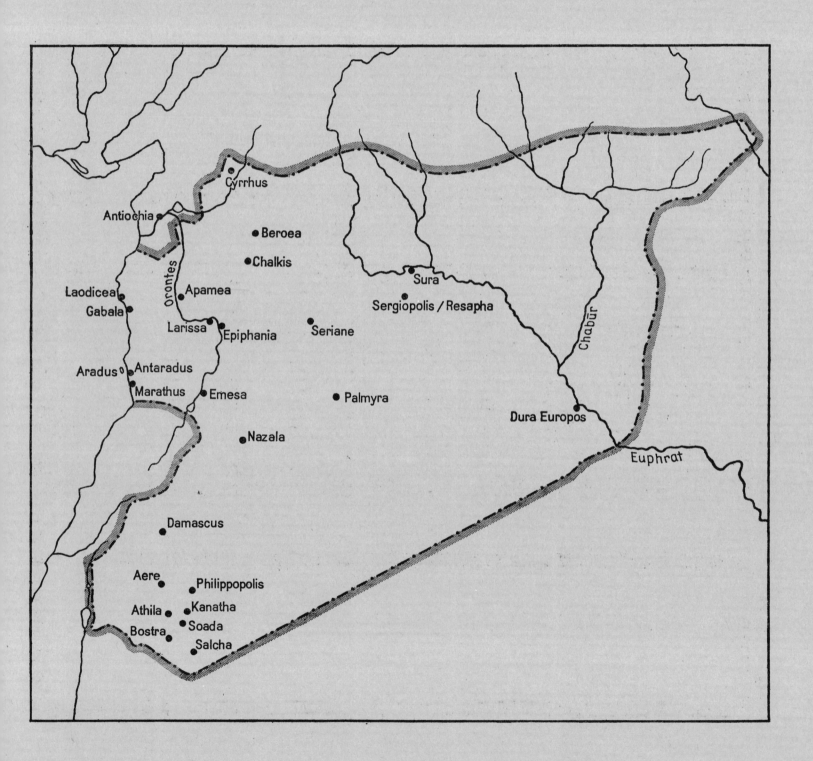

Cyrrhus

Antiochia

Beroea

Chalkis

Sura

Laodicea

Apamea

Orontes

Sergiopolis / Resapha

Gabala

Larissa

Seriane

Epiphania

Chabūr

Aradus

Antaradus

Marathus

Emesa

Palmyra

Dura Europos

Nazala

Euphrat

Damascus

Aere

Philippopolis

Athila

Kanatha

Bostra

Soada

Salcha

APAMEA (QAL'AT MUDIQ). *The pillars of the great colonnades, here seen from the south, are the most remarkable discoveries so far on this site.*

APAMEA. *Corinthian pillars on the main street, with the remains of an entablature of a portico which sheltered foot passengers from sun and rain.*

APAMEA. *From the present main street of the town one can look over the Ghab valley to the Djebel el-Anzeriye. Although these coastal mountains rise rather steeply out of the valley of the Orontes, they present no serious difficulties to traffic from Apamea to the Mediterranean; they reach heights of between 1200 and 1500 m, but slope less steeply down to the coast.*

APAMEA. *A considerable number of the Corinthian pillars which supported the roofing of the pathways at either side of the main street, and even parts of the entablature, have survived.*

DURA EUROPOS, (SALHIYE). In the southwest corner of the town there was a place sacred to the god Aphlad, revered as son of the weather god; Parthian influence in particular can be detected in this cult. The relief, 51 by 31 cm, today in the National Museum in Damascus, gives an idea of how people in Dura Europos envisaged this god. He stands on two winged mythical creatures; his outer garment is that of a Greek officer and the under-garment showing at the arms and knees is Parthian. Beside him, before a small altar, a priest offers up a sacrifice. The Greek inscription states that a certain Adadiabos, son of Zabdibolos, had the monument built for the benefit and protection of himself and his children and his entire house. The relief can be dated at about the early 1st century.

DURA EUROPOS. View of the citadel from the town. The west wall of the citadel still stands to a height of over 20 m and is 288 m long. The east side has been washed away by the Euphrates.

DURA EUROPOS. The Euphrates has dug a deep bed here, so that the desert plateau rises up steeply. At the edge of the plateau a fragment of wall can be seen which was part of the fortifications of the citadel.

APAMEA. *Pillars of the great colonnade on the cardo maximus, the main street of Apamea, which ran through the city in a north to south direction for nearly 1800 m. Statues of honoured citizens and other dignitaries once stood on the consoles of these pillars.*

DURA EUROPOS. *Dura Europos can be reached from the asphalt road which runs past the ruins on the desert plateau to the west. From this side a long wall, with fortress towers rising out of it at intervals, can be seen. The picture shows the northwest part of the wall and the breaches in it through which, until recently, the road led into the town and farther on to Abu Kemal.*

DURA EUROPOS. *View from the desert towards the so-called Palmyra Gate in the western city wall. This gate had two storeys; attackers could be shot at through narrow windows from the upper storey. The material used for the gate was shining white gypsum; mud bricks were used for most of the buildings inside the town.*

DURA EUROPOS. *A tower in the city fortifications to the northwest was incorporated in the Temple of the Palmyrean Gods; from this tower there is a view into the courtyard of the temple. Both this and the neighbouring Tower of the Archers were reinforced on the inside by walls of unburnt brick. This made them narrow inside and left no room for steps up to the second storeys, which evidently had to be reached by ladders.*

DURA EUROPOS. *View of the courtyard of the Temple of the Palmyrean Gods. In the foreground the remains of one of the pillars which stood at the entrance to the holy of holies, behind it a "kiosk" in which the figure of a god was set up. This is a small, rectangular structure built against the north wall of the courtyard with four corner pillars of which two pairs are linked together by means of parallel walls. Between these there is a niche two metres wide with a step in front of it. An image of a god probably stood here, with a lamp burning in front of it. Some faint traces of colour indicate that the structure was once painted.*

DURA EUROPOS. *The Temple of the Palmyrean Gods, a reminder of the close economic and cultural links between the fortress on the Euphrates and the oasis city of Palmyra, is in the northwest corner of the city wall. The pillars belong to the entrance hall to the cella, where the wall paintings were found which led to archaeological investigations of Dura Europos. The diameter of these simple pillars resting on quadratic bases is 82 cm.*

DURA EUROPOS. *Not far from the Temple of the Palmyrean Gods the Tower of the Archers has survived. Only fragments of the pillars which stood before it remain; they formed part of the colonnade on the square in front of the tower.*

DURA EUROPOS. *Excavations have also exposed the town's public baths. The photograph shows the cold bath (frigidarium), a rectangular room 12.75 by 10.25 m with two entrances. Six pillars stood at the edge of the bath, which was 1.48 m deep. Later on, when the bath was probably partly in ruins, an amphitheatre was built beside it.*

BOSTRA (BOSRA). *This aerial view shows the present-day Bosra esh-Sham. It is surrounded by fields marked off by walls of piled-up boulders. In the central foreground rises the citadel which was built in the 13th century round the ancient theatre. Excavations have again exposed the Roman theatre. In the background, right, a water reservoir at the southeast corner of the old city wall, which did not include the theatre within the city.*

BOSTRA. *The theatre is one of the biggest buildings of its kind in the Near East. It is especially well preserved, owing to the fact that the auditorium was filled up with earth when it was transformed into a citadel. Excavation work by the Directorate-General for Ancient Monuments and Museums has been going on here since 1947. The semi-circular auditorium has a diameter of 102 m and narrow steps gave access to 35 rows*

of seats, the front edges of which project slightly and are profiled. Two gangways divide the rows of seats into three sections and a row of plain pillars with entablatures ends the top section. Behind these there is a promenade with a broad view over the fertile Hauran plain. The stage, 45 m in length, ended in a much-divided scena front. The theatre is being re-constructed and will soon be used for performances again.

BOSTRA. *Of the city gates the west gate is the best preserved. It probably dates back to the 2nd century* A.D. *The tall gateway is spanned by two arches one above the other. The front, divided up by pilasters and niches, is built slightly forwards at the sides to form rectangular towers, each of which contains a large room. Apart from this most of the Roman city wall has disappeared. Through this gate one comes into the street which still runs straight through the city.*

BOSTRA. *The four pillars with their well-preserved Corinthian capitals still rise to a height of 14 m at the place where the main street with its colonnades crossed an important side street. The pillars were perhaps part of a nymphaeum and held up the roof of the entrance hall. Nothing more can be seen of what once lay behind this, but travellers in the 19th century saw the remains of an apse.*

BOSTRA. Two tall pillars and part of the cella wall (ante) in front of them are all that is left of the temple near the nymphaeum. A fragment of the entablature gives an impression of the rich ornamentation of this temple. The second pillar stands 24 m away from the one shown here.

BOSTRA. The main street was spanned by an arched gateway at its eastern end; there is only one entry and the façade is decorated with niches and half-pillars. Like all the other buildings, this triumphal arch was built of the dark basalt found in the Hauran region. It probably dates back to the early 2nd century.

PHILIPPOPOLIS (SHAKHBA). *The ruins of the baths (thermae) are still impressive today because of their generous lay-out. The water was brought from the mountains through an aqueduct. The east wall of the vestiarium (changing-room) can be seen through an arched doorway. The Arab dwellinghouse built in here gives a striking impression of the monumental character of the Roman building.*

PHILIPPOPOLIS. *The Roman Emperor Philippus Arabs, the founder of the city, dedicated a small temple to his deified father Julius Marinus; it is now usually called the Philippeion. An inscription at the entrance to the cella—a simple structure with corner pilasters and a few windows— provides evidence for this. The surrounding pillars have disappeared.*

PHILIPPOPOLIS. *The dark basalt paving of this Roman street is still travelled over today. Nothing is left of the colonnades which lined it. Some of the buildings in the background date back to Roman times.*

PHILIPPOPOLIS. *From the roof of the Philippeion, which can be reached by an old stone stairway in the interior, there is not only a broad view over Shakhba and its surroundings; but also over the small theatre. In the foreground, the semi-circular auditorium surrounded by a thick stone wall with entrance gates. To the left, the stage building, and at the extreme right part of the promenade, which was roofed by barrel vaulting. In the background, houses of present-day Shakhba. Parts of the ancient architecture were often used again in these buildings.*

PHILIPPOPOLIS. *The scena—the stage building facing the auditorium—is a rectangular structure 42 by 12 m. On its north side is the stage, 20 by 4.3 m. The stage front is arranged similar to a gateway: in the centre a tall entrance and on either side two smaller ones flanked by semi-circular and rectangular niches.*

83

PHILIPPOPOLIS. *The theatre, not far from the city centre, gives a good impression of what a small Roman theatre looked like. The auditorium has a diameter of 41 m and the rows of seats are divided into two tiers by a lower and upper gangway. Very little remains of the upper tier.*

PHILIPPOPOLIS. *A promenade can be seen through the entry in the semi-circular outer wall of the theatre.*

PHILIPPOPOLIS. *View from the orchestra—the space between the stage and the seats in the auditorium. To the left, the vaulted entrance to the orchestra, next to it the ten rows of seats of the lower tier and one of the sets of steps which divided the auditorium into wedge-shaped sections (carcidae). Between the lower and upper tiers— little is left of the latter—there is a promenade.*

PHILIPPOPOLIS. *The builders of the theatre were able to make use of the naturally sloping ground and built the auditorium up against it. The promenade levels up the difference in height by steps; the gangway, 2.86 m wide, was covered by barrel vaulting and could be reached from outside by five entrances.*

KANATHA (QANAWAT). *The oldest building, a Roman temple of the 2nd century, stands in the so-called seraglio, the acropolis of old Kanatha. A Christian church was built into this temple in the 5th century. The photograph shows the remains of the entrance hall of the temple. The pillars bear consoles on the outside.*

BOSTRA. *There was a big triumphal arch at the centre of the Roman city; it had three entries, the tallest 8 m in height and its north front lies along the main street. The side street leading to the south gate passed under this arch. There are consoles on the four pilasters of the north façade—not shown here. In the background, the four pillars of the nymphaeum and a pillar of the great temple.*

PHILIPPOPOLIS. *The mosaic shown here is also allegorical. It is 3.37 by 2.76 m and the colours are yellow, red, green, orange, black and blue. A group of gods and semi-gods, their names beside them in Greek letters, are framed in a geometrically patterned border. In the central foreground, Earth with her children, the geniuses of agriculture ranged behind them. Left, Aion, the genius of infinite time, with women representing the four seasons. Right, Prometheus, shaping a human being, and behind him the young Hermes with his staff. Above the group, heads look down from the clouds; these represent the winds and the dew. The mosaic, a tribute to the fertile Hauran plain, also points to trade—in the person of Hermes—and is probably one of the most important mosaics to come down to us from the ancient Near East. Damascus, National Museum.*

PHILIPPOPOLIS. *Mosaic with an allegorical picture; Eutekneia, representing "Joy with children", sits on a throne in the middle. To the left, Philosophy, in front of whom stands a basket full of parchment rolls. To the right, Justice (Dikaiosyne). The colours of the mosaic are violet, garnet, yellow and black. Damascus, National Museum.*

KANATHA. *A number of pillars with Corinthian columns still stand on the terrace of the Temple of Helios, a peripter outside the old outer wall. The cella was surrounded by 24 pillars whose tall pedestals were richly decorated. 2nd century A.D.*

KANATHA. *The oldest building in the so-called seraglio is a Roman temple of the 2nd century A.D. In the Pronaos, the entrance hall, stood Corinthian pillars with consoles on their front sides. Remains of the entablature on these pillars can still be seen.*

KANATHA. *Excavations by the Syrian Ancient Monuments Administration have exposed vaults near the seraglio which probably date back to the time when Kanatha was the seat of a bishopric. The sarcophagus is richly decorated on the front side. The Greek cross indicates the Christian faith of the dead.*

KANATHA. *The atrium in front of the basilica— 4th to 5th century A.D.—has plain pillars with rectangular plate capitals. The room clearly served as a reception hall for guests of the officials of the basilica.*

KANATHA. *The basilica could be reached from the atrium through three richly decorated doors. The view through one of the side doors gives a view of the pillars of the basilica on their high rectangular pedestals; these were once arched over.*

PANEAS (BANYAS). *An imago clipeata—shield bust—of a noble lady was found at Banyas in South Syria in 1964; the work, which has a diameter of 39 cm, dates back to the 2nd century* A.D. *Damascus, National Museum.*

KANATHA. *The Christian church built into the old Roman temple has a richly decorated central gate on its west front. The church itself is in the form of a triple-shipped basilica. Its apse was built against the east wall of the Roman temple, so that the axis of the church was at an angle of 90° to the temple. The west façade of the church projects beyond the west wall of the temple.*

KANATHA. *Remains of ancient buildings can also be found on the other side of the wadi. In the foreground, a building at the centre of which there was a spring, so that it was probably a nymphaeum. A little farther down river, no longer in the picture, the little theatre of the town was built against the slope.*

DAMASCUS (DIMASHQ). *At the eastern end of the via recta which bisects the old city stands Bab Sharqi (east gate). This is the best preserved Roman city gate in Damascus. Restoration work has been done here in recent years by the Directorate-General for Ancient Monuments and Museums of the Syrian Arab Republic, the results of which can already be seen in this picture. The gate is now in its original form with the three entrances arched over and flanked by pilasters. The gate is surmounted by a rectangular minaret of the Osman period.*

LAODICEA (LATAKIA). The tetrapylon set up about 200 A.D. is so far the only important architectural monument of Roman Laodicea known to us. Some dwellings close up against the gate have been demolished, so that it now has worthy surroundings again. The original level of the Roman streets can now be clearly seen. According to the width of the street, the entrances are 5.8 or 4.75 m in height. In the background, part of the old city of Latakia.

A network of paved roads covered Roman Syria. A section of the road leading from Antioch (Antakya) via Aleppo to Chalcis (Qinnesrin) is especially well preserved. Like many others, parts of this road were pulled up for use in later building, but it is intact for a stretch of more than a kilometre west of Aleppo. The big limestone squares were laid on the bed rock. The road was 6 m in width and was roughened on the surface to give horses' hoofs a better grip. The road was probably built in the early 2nd century, the period when the Romans did a great deal of road-building in Syria.

SOADA–DIONYSIA (SUWEDA). *One of the most interesting smaller finds in the Hauran region, an example of the art of the Roman provinces, is a statue of the goddess Minerva, patron of craftsmen, doctors and teachers. She wears a long cloak, and her shoulders and breast are protected by armour with a gorgon's head. Her armour consisted of the oval shield and helmet and a spear, now lost. The figure stands on a pedestal and is 1.6 m in height. Damascus, National Museum.*

EMESA (HOMS). *A number of pieces of jewellery and a helmet with mask which probably dates back to the first half of the 1st century A.D. were discovered in a royal necropolis west of Homs in 1940. The upper part of the helmet is iron; it is bisected by a silver band ending in a flower and surrounded by a silver wreath. The mask shows an expressive face with fleshy nose and full lips. This is also of iron but entirely covered with silver. This work of art, which is 24.5 cm in height and approaches the quality of a portrait, probably came from a Syrian workshop (Antioch?) and represents a prince. Damascus, National Museum.*

GABALA (DJEBLE). *An over-turned entablature gives an idea of the former architectonic decoration of the theatre; possibly part of the stage building.*

GABALA. *The Roman theatre in this small coastal town south of Latakia, which could accommodate about 8000 spectators, gives an impression of the former importance of the place. The big auditorium is divided into sections by steps; two promenades divide the seats into three tiers. The main entrance led through vaults to the first promenade, which is still in a good state of preservation. A kind of box in the lower tier could also be reached from here by ase parate set of steps.*

The ruins of Marathus bring us well into the period of Syrian history which we shall call Graeco-Roman. This covers about seven centuries, from Alexander the Great to the division of the Roman Empire at the end of the 4th century A.D. The Roman occupation of Syria in 64 B.C. forms an important break within this long period. But as has already been pointed out this periodisation, which is orientated around events in political history, cannot be more than an aid in dividing cultural developments in Syria into surveyable chapters. The transitions are fluid and cannot be pinned down to definite dates.

The influence of the Aegean world on Syria had begun long before Alexander started his triumphal march through the Orient, and the division of the Empire in 395 A.D. was little more than an administrative act which meant as little for Syria's socio-economic structure as for its culture. But developments which in the final analysis led to important changes were in fact favoured or ushered in by the events mentioned above as decisive for a break.

While during Syria's ancient oriental period her culture was marked by a strong polycentrism which left plenty of scope for both outside influences and also special local developments and produced a variety of forms, the Graeco-Roman emerges as a period of a more unitary character. A lively cultural life developed in the towns, especially those newly founded, with the Graeco-Macedonian upper class. This is also evident in the material objects it left behind, and especially in its architecture. Rome, which exerted its influence farther outside the city centres than the Macedonian Seleucids had done, both greatly aided the inclusion of Syria in the scope of ancient culture and also adopted a number of traditions and elements of Oriental origin. On Syrian soil the meeting of East and West led to a mutual enrichment in which it is not always easy to decide which gave the most.

Although the Graeco-Roman era was much shorter than the preceding ancient Oriental period, it has nevertheless left us many a monument. Stone was used more and more often for building purposes and has survived the centuries much better than mud-brick buildings. Thus it is still possible—thanks to the reconstruction work done by the Syrian Ancient Monuments Administration—to walk along old paved streets between colonnades and tall ancient buildings.

When Alexander the Great conquered Syria after the Battle of Issos (333 B.C.) he left the country a united province as it had been under the Persians. Only the trans-Euphrates area was separated and went more and more its own way in historical development; it was less strongly influenced by Hellenism than Syria west of the river. Of Alexander's successors who fought for his possessions, Antigonos first succeeded in gaining control of Syria, but lost it in 301 to Seleucos. Syria came under Seleucid rule as far as the valley of Homs, and Seleucos and his heirs called themselves Kings of Syria from that time on. The land south of the River Eleutheros (Nahr el-Kebir) continued to be occupied by the Egyptian Ptolemies. The conflicts between the Seleucids and the Ptolemies finally ended about 200 B.C. with the inclusion of southern Syria under Seleucid rule. A whole series of cities owed their foundation or—in the case of older settlements—their expansion to the Seleucids. Antioch became the capital (today the Turkish Antakya), but along with it other cities like Apamea, Laodicea and Dura Europos increased in importance. A lively economic and cultural life developed there, but the surrounding plains were little affected. The Seleucids did not succeed in welding their territories into a genuine entity: political confusion, in which kings fought against kings, the efforts of the cities and local princes to become independent, and also the advance of the Parthians to the Euphrates weakened Seleucid Syria and delivered it up to King Tigranes II of Armenia (83 B.C.) and later to the Romans (64 B.C.).

When Syria was transformed into a Roman province under Pompey in 63 A.D. the southeastern regions and Palmyra remained outside. The Arab Nabataeans, who also ruled the Hauran region from their capital Petra, at times spread their influence even as far as Damascus. The Romans gradually succeeded in setting aside the native dynasties and using this region as a buffer against the Parthians of Mesopotamia and the Arab Bedouin tribes. In 106 A.D. the imperial governor of Syria, A. Cornelius Palma, transformed the northern part of the Nabataean state into the Roman province of Arabia, whose centre was Bostra (Bosra esh-Sham) in the southern Hauran region. Territories won east of the Euphrates came under the province of Mesopotamia. A further change in the distribution of provinces was undertaken under the Emperor Septimius Severus in 195 A.D. In order to limit the power of the imperial governors of this rich province, Syria was divided into Syria Coele and—from the Lebanese coast to Palmyra—Syria Phoenice. Palmyra had in the meantime been incorporated into the Empire. The most southerly regions of Syria were included in the provinces of Arabia and Palestine.

A whole series of cities in Syria were newly founded or much expanded in Roman times, their image being typically Roman. The remains of these cities can be found in many places, and we cannot deal with anything like all of them here. Much of what impressed travellers in the late Middle Ages has remained standing throughout the centuries, and much has also been rescued by archaeological excavations.

The Graeco-Roman city generally emerges as a more or less regular square with city gates approximately in the middle of each wall. A main street with pillared pathways on either side led straight through the city, and at the crossing with the most important side streets there was often a kind of gateway with four pillars, a tetrapylon. Architectonically outstanding buildings were the temple and smaller sanctuaries, such as the Nymphea (sacred springs) as well as baths, theatres and residences of the Roman officials.

Agriculture was the main reason for the rise of these cities. Syria was regarded as one of the granaries of the Roman Empire and a geographical description of Syria in the 4th century as a country with "a superfluity of grain, wine and oil" was certainly not an exaggeration. In addition to agricultural products, Syria also produced glass and linen, and in the end its position on the trade routes brought big profits; even Chinese raw silk came into the country. The Romans tried to protect this important province by a frontier wall, a limes, which ran right through the Syrian desert and Upper Mesopotamia. There are still some remains of the fortresses set up along this wall in the reign of the Emperor Diocletian. A network of roads was built for purposes of trade, but also for military reasons. The roads from ancient oriental and Greek times were rebuilt in accordance with the latest technical standards, paved and often even supplied with milestones, and other roads were newly built (Page 97). Good roads led from the capital, Antioch, through Laodicea (Latakia) and Antaradus (Tartus) to Ptolemais south of Tyrus and through Apamea and Emesa (Homs) to Heliopolis (Baalbek). Other roads led to the Upper Euphrates and the middle reaches of the river. Apamea was the starting point for roads to Chalcis (Qinnesrin) in North Syria, to Palmyra and to Antaradus. The important city of Cyrrhus in the far north could be reached by good roads from the Euphrates and Central Syria and an important road led from Samosata on the Euphrates downstream to Sura (el-Hammam). From Sura a road branched off to Sergiopolis (Rusafa) and Palmyra and continued through Nazala (Karyatan) to Damascus. The famous Strata Diocletiana later took this route, which turned south before Damascus and continued as far as the Hauran region. The Syrian roads were part of an over-all network which covered the Roman Near East and made travelling easier for trade caravans as well as increasing the mobility of the army.

APAMEA (QAL'AT MUDIQ)

Ancient Apamea or, as in Greek texts, Apameia, lies about 20 km west of Khan Shekhun, not far from the Damascus-Aleppo road. It is a widespread site in which so far only a small part of the ruins have been laid bare, on the edge of the Orontes valley, which here broadens out to form the Ghab plain and ends in the west with the steeply rising coastal mountains (Page 66). Where the citadel of Apamea rises above the town and the plain, lies the Arab village of Qal'at Mudiq (Page 15), whose ring wall dates from the 13th century, the end of the Crusades. It is clear from its favourable position on the edge of the broad plain and on the old north-south route through the Syrian hinterland that this place must have been settled in ancient oriental times. Cuneiform texts of the 2nd millennium B.C. indicate that the city of Niya may have been here. It cannot yet be stated with certainty whether this Bronze Age settlement—for some time the centre of a kingdom—lies under the citadel of Apamea and the present village of Qal'at Mudiq. Tuthmosis I and Tuthmosis III of Egypt hunted the later extinct Syrian elephant in the Land of Niya in the middle of the 2nd millennium B.C.; the partially marshy Ghab valley was apparently a favourable habitat for the Syrian elephant. But Apamea only rose to importance in Graeco-Roman times.

When Alexander the Great occupied the place, at that time called Pharnaka, he renamed it Pella in memory of his father's birthplace in Macedonia. Seleucos I (321–281), ruler of Syria from 301 B.C., fortified and enlarged the town and named it Apameia in honour of the Persian princess whom he had married in Susa while he was still an officer in Alexander's army. This name survived for a long time—as Apamea in Roman times, Afamia during the Crusades and the time of the Islamic Arabs—until the 17th century, when the place on the site of the former citadel was re-named Qal'at Mudiq.

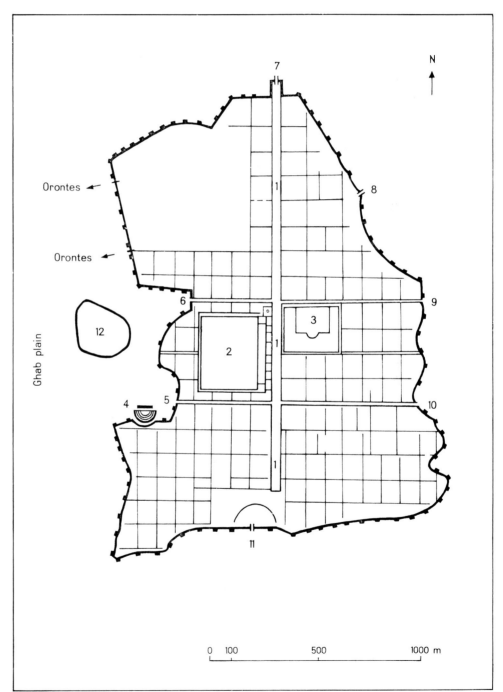

APAMEA. *Simplified map of the city. After H. Lacoste,* Bulletin de l'Académie Royale de Belgique *43 (1961), Plate I.*

Orontes ←

Orontes ←

Ghab plain

N

1 Cardo maximus
2 Agora
3 Thermae
4 Theatre
5 Sedjar (Larissa) Gate
6 Laodicea Gate
7 Antioch Gate
8 Chalcis Gate
9 Seriane Gate
10 Palmyra Gate
11 Epiphania (Hama) Gate
12 Citadel

0   100   500   1000 m

The Seleucids stationed most of their army horses in Apamea, and their war elephants are also said to have been kept there. The Roman general Pompey conquered the town in 64 A.D. and destroyed the citadel, but it soon began to flourish again and had a population which justifies us in calling Apamea an ancient city. It was the seat of a bishop in Byzantine times, but its importance gradually declined. The shifting of the trade routes hastened this decline which was finally completed when Khosraus I of Persia conquered it in 540. Earthquakes and stone quarrying hastened the disappearance of the remains of the city.

We owe the excavation and reconstruction of Apamea to a Belgian expedition in particular. When this work is finished—although it will hardly be possible or useful to excavate the entire ancient city, since farming is now done on parts of it—Apamea will without doubt be one of the most impressive sites in the Syrian Arab Republic.

The city was founded about 100 metres above the level of the Ghab plain and was surrounded by a wall about 6.3 km in length. There were seven entrance gates; these opened on to the roads leading to Antioch, Laodicea, Larissa (Sedjar), Epiphania (Hama), Palmyra, Seriane (Esriye) and Chalcis (Qinnesrin). The city itself was divided into rectangular residential areas (insulae) by sixteen roads running from south to north and east to west. The main street between the great north gate (Antioch Gate) and the south gate (Epiphania Gate) was 1774 m long and sloped downwards about 10 m, since the city sloped slightly to the south. It was 37 m wide, including the colonnades along either side, parts of which still remain. The Corinthian

pillars supported consoles on which stood statues of prominent citizens and dignitaries (Pages 65–67, 70, 71). This main street, the "cardo maximus", was intersected by two important cross streets which also ran from gate to gate. The southerly one, which was 1150 m long, also had colonnades on either side. The other, smaller streets were about 6 m wide. The agora, a big rectangular assembly square, was in the centre of the city close to the main street. The public baths stood opposite. The huge theatre, not yet completely excavated, was outside the city walls and here the slope towards the Ghab plain was taken advantage of. With its 145 m long facade it is one of the biggest theatre buildings of the Roman period. From its rows of seats the audience had a broad view of the Ghab valley and the high-lying citadel. The beauty of the surrounding landscape will not fail to make a deep impression on future visitors to the reconstructed theatre, in which it is planned to present drama again.

DURA EUROPOS (SALHIYE)

In March 1921 an English officer occupying the hill of Salhiye on the Euphrates with his troops reported the discovery of "wall paintings in a wonderful state of preservation". When the archaeological expedition under the American J. H. Breasted arrived there, however, he had only one day to examine the finds, for the British troops had in the meantime received orders to abandon the hill. But the discovery of the paintings and the brief examination of them by J. H. Breasted aroused archaeological interest in this site, which travellers had already visited many times. In 1922 and 1923 a French expedition under

DURA EUROPOS. *Simplified city map with the most important buildings. After A. Detweiler (1935) in: M. I. Rostovtzeff, The Excavations at Dura Europos, 9th Season (New Haven 1944), Appendix.*

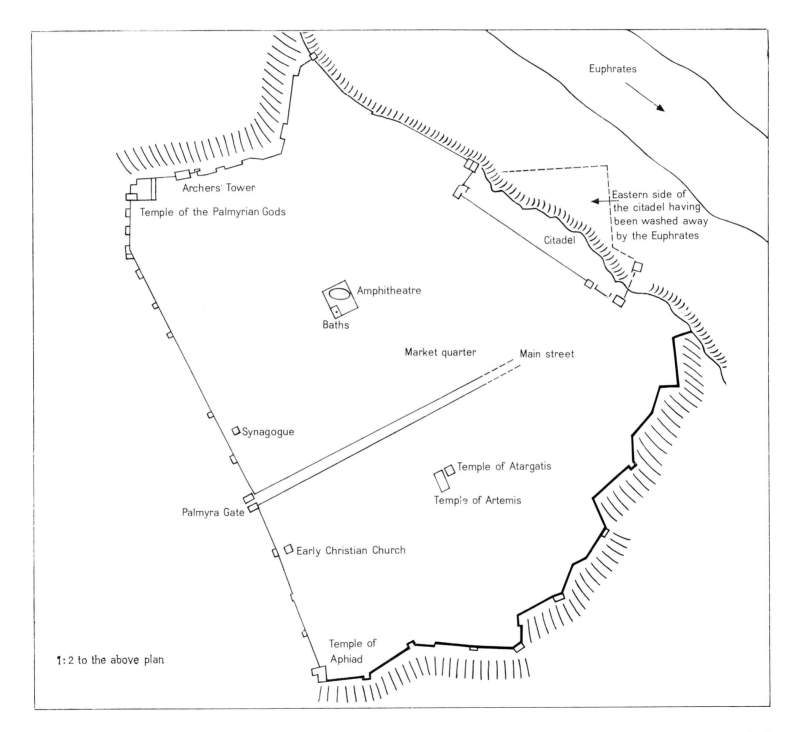

Euphrates

Archers' Tower

Temple of the Palmyrian Gods

Eastern side of
the citadel having
been washed away
by the Euphrates

Citadel

Amphitheatre

Baths

Market quarter   Main street

Synagogue

Temple of Atargatis

Temple of Artemis

Palmyra Gate

Early Christian Church

Temple of
Aphiad

1:2 to the above plan

F. Cumont conducted excavations at Salhiye on the site of ancient Dura Europos (then part of French mandated Syria). Work was continued from 1928 to 1936 by an American-French team under M.Pillet. The results, especially the well-preserved wall paintings and the numerous inscriptions in Greek, Latin and Palmyrian, fully justified the long years of work done by archaeologists. The huge site, which covers 73 hectares (about 160 acres), still offers broad scope for further investigations.

Dura Europos owes its origin and its golden age especially to its favourable position: it is on the edge of the steep drop from the desert to the valley of the Euphrates, commanded the trade routes running along the river and thus shared in the trade which flowed between the countries on the Persian Gulf and the Mediterranean. From its position Dura Europos was the successor of ancient Mari, already destroyed in the 18th century B.C., which had flourished a little farther south on the Euphrates. The terrain was also suitable for the building of a fortress: in the east, north and south the land falls steeply away, so that this natural defence position needed only to be closed off by walls. Directly on the river there was a high rock suitable for a citadel. The city had to be specially well fortified to the west, facing the Syrian desert. This task was already undertaken under the first of the Seleucid rulers, Seleucos I. Nikanor, one of the king's generals, built a fortress at the end of the 4th century B.C. and named it after Europos, the birthplace of Seleucos in Macedonia. "Dur(a)", the old Semitic word for fortress was placed before it. Another name is found in inscriptions: Dura Nikanoris—Nikanor's fortress.

Despite the numerous inscriptions found at Dura Europos and a very frequent mention of it in written sources of other origin, its political history cannot be given in detail. Since Dura Europos was first in the Seleucid-Parthian, then in the Roman-Parthian and finally in the Roman-Sassanid frontier region, and the legal position often changed, its fate also varied. The Seleucid fortress was captured by the Parthians at the end of the 2nd century B.C. and they held it even after the Romans had occupied the rest of Syria west of the Euphrates and turned it into a Roman province. The Romans succeeded in gaining a firm footing here only after the mid-2nd century A.D., but even then they had to fight for their possessions repeatedly against the Parthians. Dura Europos was captured by the Persian Sassanids about the middle of the 3rd century A.D., but these soon had to give way to the Palmyrians, who in turn withdrew when their own capital was attacked by the Romans (about 272). The city again fell into the hands of the Sassanids but thereafter gradually collapsed in ruins and in 363, somewhat more than a hundred years after the end of Roman occupation, only the "remains of what had once been a city" could be seen. The place was never again settled. It lay far away from the main theatre of historical developments and it was not worth while to re-found it.

The road linking Der es-Zor with the frontier town Abu Kemal led until quite recently right through Dura Europos. Today it runs somewhat west of it. Approaching the ruins from the road, one first sees the long west wall fortified by towers which protected the city from attacks from the desert plateau (Page 72). In their midst rises a big gateway,

the former only entrance to the city from the desert side which excavators call the Palmyra Gate because of its position (Page 72). The main street of Dura Europos began here; it broadened to a width of 14.3 m and led through covered bazaars to the Euphrates side. A temple was excavated in the northwest corner of the city, the so-called Temple of the Palmyrian Gods, which was dedicated to the three deities of Palmyra, also worshipped here on the Euphrates. The wall paintings in this temple were those discovered by the English officer in 1921 which drew attention to Dura Europos.

The temple is connected with the city wall by a tower (Page 73), it has been a rectangular courtyard (Page 74) surrounded by a number of rooms. The temple proper lay to the west; it had an ante-room of which four pillars still remain (Page 74). In the cella, the sanctum, there was a semi-circular structure which opened towards the entrance and showed the place where the pictures of the deities stood. The walls were covered with paintings, of which those on the south wall have become best known. They depict a sacrificial ceremony: Konon, son of Nicostrates, together with two priests, conducts a sacrifice in the presence of his entire family. In his hands he holds a rose-coloured band with blue ends and a cord; the horns of the sacrificial animal may have been decorated with these. Somewhat in the foreground stands a priest clad in a tall white hat and a long white robe in front of a blue fayence vase in which he is dipping a twig. In his left hand he holds a sacrificial dish and a jug, both of blue fayence. Two daggers can be seen on the dish; these were used to kill the sacrificial animal. Beside him stands another

Palmyrian priest, in front of whom there is an incense altar and the rest of Konon's family who are attending the ceremony.

Of the other buildings laid bare during excavations at Dura Europos, mention should be made of a synagogue and an early Christian church, both on the western city wall and decorated with interesting wall paintings, and of the Archers' Tower *(Page 75)*, the agora and the bazaar. The frescoes from the synagogue are now one of the main attractions in the National Museum in Damascus. Both the church and the synagogue were the victims when the city walls were strengthened to defend the Roman fortress against the Sassanids. The lane and the houses behind were filled in with rubble, but for this very reason the paintings have come down to us so well preserved. The agora, the bazaar, the temples of Artemis, Atargatis and other deities *(Page 68)*, many rectangular houses, baths *(Page 75)*, an amphitheatre and cross-roads were also excavated. Of the citadel rising up on the rocks by the Euphrates, a long wall with three gates protected by towers *(Page 69)* facing towards the city can still be seen. The eastern side has been washed away by the river, which has changed its course several times *(Page 69)*.

The single finds, dating back to Greek, Parthian and Roman times, are numerous. Amongst the objects excavated are reliefs of gods, statues, consecrated altars, pottery (terracotta) figures, glass and ceramics, plaited shields and remains of fabrics, a set of bronze harness, coins and the like. These are evidences of every-day life, of cults and warfare techniques which fill out the architectonic picture of the city and clearly show that Dura Europos remained very much an orien-

tal city in spite of many Graeco-Roman forms.

Apamea and Dura Europos are examples of Seleucid foundations which still flourished under Roman rule. Other places flourished first in the Roman era—for example, those in the far south of the Syrian Arab Republic, in the fertile Hauran plain and in Djebel Druz. This region is rich in monuments of Syrian antiquity *(Page 108)*. The lava soil of the Hauran plain produced good corn harvests and this made it one of the granaries of the Roman Empire. Three main factors constituted a threat to this region with its natural wealth: plundering Bedouin tribes, swarms of locusts and drought. The protection which the Roman army was able to give the Hauran did away to a considerable extent with the first factor and thus contributed to the flourishing of the region.

It is still not possible to determine exactly how far the Hauran was settled in ancient oriental times. A number of place names which could be localised here, as well as the fertility of the soil, suggest that there were at least periodical settlements whose inhabitants led a nomadic life. Before the region was occupied by the Romans and its southern part incorporated into the province of Arabia, founded in 106 A.D., it belonged to the Kingdom of the Arab Nabataeans of Petra. Little remains of this pre-Roman period; much is certainly covered by ruins of the Roman era, which are all the more numerous. In Sanamen, the old Aere, remains of a temple built in 191 A.D., are still standing, and in Inkhil, somewhat south of this, an ancient villa built in the same century can still be seen. The district capital of Suweda, old Soada or Dionysia, still has the remains

DURA EUROPOS. *Wall painting from the temple of the Palmyrean gods, section: Konon and two priests offering up a sacrifice. C. 75 B.C. National Museum, Damascus. After a photograph in the National Museum.*

of a number of ancient buildings and is a source of interesting small monuments *(cf. Page 98)*. In Sia (Seia), in addition to the ruins of several Roman temples, there are remains of an older temple of Baalshamin, the Semitic Ruler of Heaven. One of the two temples of 'Atil (Athila) was built in 151 A.D. in the reign of the Emperor Antonius Pius, that in Mushennef (Nela) somewhat later. The remains of Roman dwellings as well as impressive ruins of the Byzantine era are of interest in Shaqqa, the ancient Sakkeia or Maximilianopolis, and the citadel of Salkhad (Salkha) in the southern Hauran dates back to Nabataean times and was rebuilt under Islam. These few examples may suffice to indicate the wealth of ancient monuments in the Hauran region. The three most important centres of Roman antiquity in Hauran, Bosra, Qanawat and Shakhba will be described in more detail.

BOSTRA (BOSRA ESH-SHAM)

Bosra lies in the southwestern foot-hills of Djebel Druz in a fertile valley about 800 m above sea level *(Page 76)*. The royal residence of Busruna mentioned in cuneiform texts probably stood on this site in the Bronze Age—in the 2nd millennium. Bosra first appears in written sources a thousand years later. Alexander the Great conquered the place. In the early 1st century B.C., when the power of the Seleucids was already declining, the Arab Nabataeans of Petra pushed far to the north. The king of the Nabataeans succeeded in extending his rule to the oasis of Damascus. Bosra, situated at a strategically and economically important point, was built up into a fortress which was intended to

DURA EUROPOS. *Graffito of the so-called Palmyra Gate. After M.I. Rostovtzeff, The Excavations at Dura Europos, 5th Season (New Haven 1934), Plate XXXIII, 1.*

safeguard the fertile Hauran valley against invasion by nomad tribes. When the Romans conquered Syria Bosra remained in the hands of the Nabataeans and was then on their northern frontier facing the Roman province of Syria until, in 106 A.D., the Romans destroyed the Kingdom of Nabataea under the order of the Emperor Trajan and included the northern part of it directly in the Roman Empire as the province of Arabia. Bosra now received the name Nova Trajana Bostra and became the centre and capital of this province, on account of its favourable position and importance. Its economic existence was based on the fertility of the surrounding region, on its role as a market for the Bedouins of the desert regions to the east and especially on its position to the trade routes. The caravan routes from Damascus to the Red Sea and from the Mediterranean through the Syrian desert to the Persian Gulf crossed at Bostra. Five paved roads met here and made Bostra an important transport centre. The city was also well supplied with water; there were a number of springs, big reservoirs stored rain water and melting snow came down in abundance from the Djebel Druz in spring. The fall of the former Nabataean capital of Petra (southeast of the Dead Sea) favoured the rise of Bostra, which was able to take over part of Petra's trade. Bostra was honoured a number of times: under Alexander Severus (222–235) it was raised to the status of a colony, it was named a metropolis by Philippus Arabs (244–249), who came from the Hauran himself. Bostra introduced its own chronology, its own era, dating from the establishment of the Province of Arabia in 106, and minted its own coins. As the seat of a bishopric, and later even of an archbishopric, it also played

a role in the Christian Byzantine period. In the 6th century one of the biggest Christian cathedrals of the Near East was built here. According to a legend, the Prophet Mohammed once visited the city when he was still a merchant. The old mosques and the citadel set up in the 13th century are signs of the importance of the place in Arab Islamic times, too. The hosts of pilgrims coming from the north to visit Mecca halted at Bostra. Later on, however, when there was no state power strong enough to protect the Hauran region, the old enemies of the settled peasants appeared again—the Bedouin tribes of the Syrian desert. They attacked the merchants' caravans and pilgrims to Mecca, who then preferred to travel along a road somewhat farther to the west. Thus Bostra lost direct contact with trade and it declined more and more as a result of this and of the constant attacks by Bedouins. The once populous city became a village whose inhabitants lived in what was left of the buildings erected in the Roman and early Christian era. Only in our own day has Bostra begun to take on new life again.

The monuments of Roman times are especially impressive in Bosra. The buildings of dark basalt, which stand out in sharp contrast to the greens and yellows of the landscape and sometimes evoke a gloomy impression, are reminders of the golden age in which the city was one of the biggest in the Roman Empire. A huge theatre dating back to the early 2nd century A.D.—the early days of the Roman province of Arabia—indicates how populous Bosra and its surroundings were. In the 13th century, the period of Arab victories over the Christian crusaders, the theatre was turned into a fortress, the auditorium

filled up with earth to form a plateau and the whole provided with a bastion for which some of the elements of the ancient building were used.

The extensive excavations undertaken since 1947 by the Directorate-General for Ancient Monuments and Museums have again exposed this theatre building, which can be considered one of the biggest and best preserved objects of its kind in the entire Orient *(Page 77)*. The cavea, the semi-circle of spectators' seats, is more than 100 m in diameter and the thirty-five rows of seats are divided up into a number of tiers by aisles and steps to form wedge-shaped sections (carcidae). The excellently preserved entrances in the lower part of the theatre were so wide that audiences could surge in and out quickly. The front of the stage is magnificently proportioned and has a row of niches, Corinthian pillars and—above these—Doric columns. These are now being set up again, after some repair work. Boxes were excavated at either side of the stage from which prominent people watched performances. The acoustics in this enormous structure are so good even today that normal speech on the stage can be clearly heard right up to the top row of seats. After restoration, performances will again be held here; this will certainly be a special experience for visitors.

Like the theatre at Apamea, this one is also outside the old Roman wall, which consists partly of the older Nabataean fortifications. The site is approximately rectangular in shape and the city wall—about 4 m thick— are broken by four main gates, one on each side, provided with tower-like projections. The western gate is especially well preserved *(Page 78)*; it dates back to the second century

A.D. It leads into the main street which bisected the city from west to east. About in the
middle of this street there is a big gate with a
triumphal arch and a broad road passing
under it, and two smaller arched side gates
(Page 88). At the crossing with the most important side street—a little farther west—
four tall Corinthian pillars can be seen which
were probably part of a sacred spring, a
nymphaeum *(Page 78)*. Travellers at the end
of the 19th century still saw many remains of
other buildings, so that the site can be fairly
completely visualised. Opposite the nymphaeum there are the remains of a temple
—two tall Corinthian pillars with part of the
architrave *(Page 79)*. Following the main
street eastwards—it had colonnades on either
side—we come to a smaller gateway, now
reconstructed, which arches over the street
(Page 79). In addition to these important
architectural monuments of ancient Bostra
mention should also be made of the market
and the remains of a palace-like structure
in which the Roman governors probably
resided. In search of evidence of Roman and
of Eastern Roman Byzantine antiquity one
encounters at every step fragments of architecture built into later dwellings and Roman
paving. From the architectural point of view,
only two other sites—Shakhba and Qanawat
in southern Syria—can be compared with
Bostra.

PHILIPPOPOLIS (SHAKHBA)

Shakhba lies at the edge of the Druz mountains at about 1050 m above sea level, on the
eastern road linking the provincial capital
Suweda with Damascus. It was founded by
the Emperor Philippus Arabs about the

DURA EUROPOS. *Reconstruction of the house of
the Roman scribes; in the background, right, the
synagogue, left, the west city wall with a tower.
After H. Pearson, in: M. I. Rostovtzeff, The Excavations at Dura Europos, 6th Season (New
Haven 1936), Plate X.*

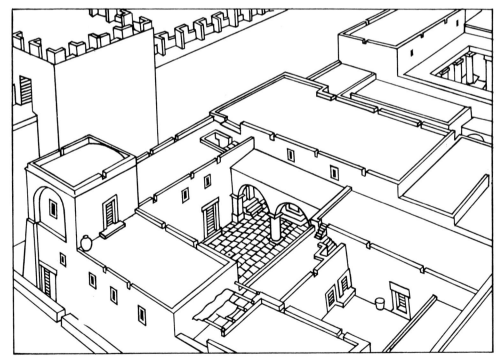

middle of the 3rd century A.D. and was given the name Philippopolis. It was built according to the typical Roman plan; the surrounding wall was an irregular rectangle and each side had a city gate in it. There were additional gates on the north and south sides of the city, of which the south gate is the best preserved. Since it was re-built it again serves as entry to the city *(Page 81)*. The main street, once lined by colonnades, runs straight through the city to the north gate and parts of it still have the old Roman basalt paving *(Page 82)*. In the most important side street, too, the paving is so well preserved that it is used today. Where these two streets cross there was a tetrapylon, very little of which remains, however. In front of this, to the right, are the public baths *(thermae)* of old Philippopolis *(Page 80)*, which got their water through an aqueduct from the mountain; a few arches belonging to this aqueduct can still be seen today. The generously planned baths included the usual changing-rooms, hot and cold baths, a medium temperature pool and, possibly, a special section for women. Most of the rooms had barrel-vaulted roofs. Not far from the baths a house with magnificent mosaics was discovered, in the southeast residential area. These works of art, which we owe to the excavations by M. Dunand, are now in the National Museum in Damascus *(Pages 89, 90)*.

Turning west from the tetrapylon into the paved street, one's attention is caught by some pillars, remains of a temple of which the terrace and some sections of wall can also still be seen. In this street, too, lie the ruins of a palace-like building whose great apse is especially noteworthy. To the left of this is the Philippeion, a small, well-preserved

BOSTRA. *Reconstruction of the east triumphal arch. After H. C. Butler (with slight alterations), Southern Syria, in: Syria. Publications of the Princeton University Archaeological Expeditions to Syria in 1904–5 and 1909, Div. II: Architecture (Leyden 1919), p. 242.*

III

temple dedicated by Philippus Arabs to the memory of his deified father; inscriptions at the entrance to the building confirm this *(Page 82)*. The Emperor's father, Julius Marinus, had lived as a sheikh in the Shakhba region. From the roof of the Philippeion there is a fine panoramic view of the little place, with its houses built mainly of dark local basalt, and of the rolling foothills of the mountains. The lay-out of the little theatre of Shakhba can also be easily surveyed from here *(Page 83)*. It stands next to the Philippeion and, since it was restored, gives a good impression of what a small Roman theatre looked like. It cannot be compared with those in Bosra and Apamea, but is of special interest because of the intimate atmosphere it conveys *(Pages 83–87)*. The diameter of the auditorium is not more than 40 m and there were probably 15 to 20 rows of seats. The stage, with its scena building divided up by arched doorways and niches, the entrances and the lower gallery and circle are so well preserved that performances could be given here today.

KANATHA (QANAWAT)

While Bostra and Shakhba lie at the foot of the Druz, we must penetrate far into the mountains to visit Qanawat. Although the highest peak here is more than 1800 m it does not rise majestically above its surroundings: on the one hand, the Hauran plain itself is between 500 and 1000 m above sea level, and on the other hand the mountains do not rise steeply at once. Qanawat can be reached by a fairly good road from Suweda, about 7 km away, and it is well worth while to make the trip on foot, because of the oak woods and

BOSTRA. *Attempt at a reconstruction of the Nymphaeum (?) on the main street of the city. After H. C. Butler, ibid., p. 253.*

the broad view over the Hauran plain with its many little villages. Qanawat itself, today a village inhabited mainly by Druses, is picturesquely situated at about 1200 m above sea level. A mountain stream has dug a deep bed here.

It can only be surmised that there had already been a settlement on the site of ancient Kanatha. During the 1st century A.D.—that is, before the province of Arabia was founded —the region is said to have been inhabited by "wild tribes" who knew neither agriculture nor towns and were supposed to hide their livestock in caves. An edict of King Herodes Agrippa of Judaea, fragments of which were discovered at Qanawat, called upon these people to abandon their "animal condition" and begin a civilised life. Troops of the Judaean king were then defeated and driven out by the Arabs near Qanawat. Kanatha-Qanawat first began to play a role, however, under Emperor Trajan (98–117), in whose reign the province of Arabia was organised and the nomadic tribes pushed back. Kanatha belonged first to the province of Syria and only towards the end of the 3rd century to the province of Arabia. The ancient buildings which can be seen at Qanawat today date back to post-Trajan days and far into the Byzantine period, when Kanatha was the seat of a Christian bishopric. In 637 Qanawat became Mohammedan—that is, later than Damascus. Far from the great roads, it gradually declined in importance.

The Roman buildings at Qanawat originated for the most part in the 2nd century A.D. Other monuments can be dated 4th or 5th century. Archaeological investigations and reconstruction work by the Syrian Ancient Monuments Administration provide an increasingly clear picture of ancient Kanatha. Outside the walls round the Roman settlement lay a temple of which the foundations and some Corinthian pillars on high pedestals have survived. This temple, whose cella is surrounded by pillars, was clearly dedicated to the sun-god Helios *(Page 91)*. In the city itself—apart from the temple of Zeus—the so-called seraglio buildings are of special interest. These are in the highest part of the city. The complex of buildings includes a Roman temple of the 2nd century *(Pages 88, 91)* into which a Christian church was built at a later date *(Pages 95, 114)*, and a 4th or 5th century basilica with a big atrium and an entrance hall *(Pages 92, 93)*. Dwelling-houses and vaults dating back to the Christian-Byzantine period, with richly ornamented sarcophagi were laid bare near this group of buildings *(Page 92)*. Ruins can also be seen on the other bank of the river Qanawat, outside Kanatha itself; these include a small theatre on the eastern slope of the wadi, an odeum and, a little farther up the river, a rectangular building with a nymphaeum at the centre *(Page 96)*.

These three south Syrian sites have left so many and such well-preserved monuments of the Roman period—for Central Syria a discovery in a grave near Homs may serve as an example *(Page 99)*—because they were not built over and thus covered by a modern settlement later on. People who settled here in post-Byzantine times built themselves dwellings amongst the ancient ruins; parts were destroyed in this way, but other buildings have survived down to our own times. Pre-Islamic architectural monuments experienced another fate, however, where the cities not only retained but were also able to increase their importance. These grew up over the remains of the ancient settlements, spread beyond them and thus set limits to archaeological research, which will have to respect later building. In such places very little—but often very impressive—evidence of ancient architecture survived.

Brief mention will be made of only three such places: the capital Damascus, the harbour city of Latakia and the little fishing harbour of Djeble.

DAMASCUS (DIMASHQ, DAMASKUS)

The name Damascus in a similar form—Timashqi—appears in written sources as early as the middle of the 2nd millennium B.C., and we know that in the early 1st millennium Damascus was the residence of an Aramaic prince who succeeded for a time in spreading his influence over large parts of Syria. We can only make an approximate guess at what Damascus looked like in ancient time, for important buildings of the Middle Ages or a later period now stand on this site. Only occasionally do building operations permit a glimpse of what is beneath. At all events, Roman Damascus lay on the site of the present Old City, which is still partly surrounded by a wall whose origin can be traced back to Roman times. The street which still runs straight across the old city is the "via recta" mentioned in the New Testament (Acts of the Apostles, IX, 11: "the street which is called straight"). It was lined by colonnades of which nothing more can be seen. In 1947 a Roman arch was discovered about 4.25 m under the present street level, excavated and set up on the present street. Since it was not broad enough to cover the

13-m-wide street it was probably over the north colonnade, whose measurements would correspond with the pillar's inner measurements. About 250 m west of this, the remains of another gate-house were found. To the east this "straight street" ended at the city gate, as it does today—at Bab Sharqi (east gate); it is now being reconstructed as it was in Roman times *(Page 96)*. The middle arch of this gate corresponds to the width of the street, the side arches led into the colonnades. In Osman times a minaret was built over the gate. Of the Roman necropolises which surrounded the city, a number of burial places in vaults with simple stone sarcophagae have recently been laid bare west of the Old City.

Certainly the most important remains of Roman Damascus are in the region of the great Omayyad Mosque, that magnificent temple in the heart of the Old City which is of great importance in art history. The place on which the 8th century mosque was built—this is one of the oldest Mohammedan mosques—was already regarded as sacred in early antiquity. Here stood the temple of the old Semitic weather god Hadad mentioned in Aramaic inscriptions, upon whose rain-dispensing favours the population of the Syrian hinterland were so dependent. At the same spot, making use for the new cult of the existing respect for the place, the Romans built a temple to Jupiter, who was placed on the same level as the ancient Hadad or Baal. A part of the surrounding wall has survived here; there was a portico along the inner side of it. Part of the ancient gable supported by six Corinthian pillars 16 m in height can still be seen where the Suq Hampiye—always filled with noise and crowds—

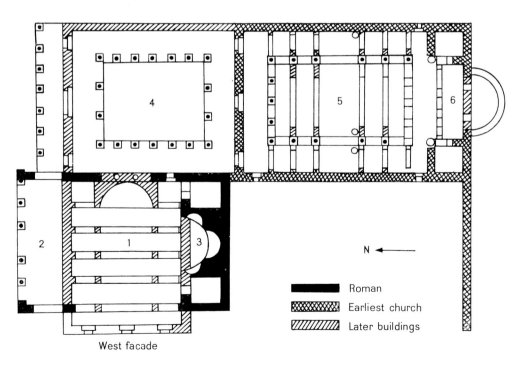

KANATHA. *Buildings of the "seraglio", ground plan. After M. de Vogué, in: R.E. Brünnow— A. von Domaszewski, Die Provincia Arabia, Vol. 3 (Strasbourg 1909), p. 118, Fig. 1014.*

1 *Church*
2 *Temple pronaos*
3 *Temple apsis*
4 *Atrium*
5 *Basilica*
6 *Choir*

West facade

N ←

■ Roman
▨ Earliest church
▨ Later buildings

approaches the Omayyad mosque. The architectural remains were part of the west gate of the enclosure; trade goes on here today as it did then. The mosque wall itself is the actual outer wall of the ancient temple. It encloses a rectangle of about 155 by 100 m. The outside wall, decorated with pilasters, probably dates back to the 3rd century A.D. The main entrance to the temple area was on the east side with monumental propylaeae in front of it. The colonnade which followed the inner side of the wall has disappeared today. It was replaced by the portico of the Omayyad mosque. Only single Corinthian pillars, used again in building the mosque, provide evidence of the colonnade of the temple of Jupiter. Nothing remains of the temple itself, which stood within this double enclosure. It was partly destroyed under Emperor Theodosius at the end of the 4th century and then converted into a triple-naved Christian basilica built up against the south wall. Transformation into a mosque then took place in the 8th century. The place has thus remained sacred for thousands of years; excavations here might lead back to the Bronze Age, to the 2nd millennium B.C.

LAODICEA (LATAKIA)

Laodicea, founded by Seleucos I at the end of the 4th century B.C. on the site of an older settlement, was also an important place in the Roman era. Later over-shadowed by other coastal towns, it has recently taken a new lease of life as one of the most important harbours of the Syrian Arab Republic. This modern town lies above the remains of the Graeco-Roman settlement, so that almost nothing can be seen of the ancient city. Only traces remain of a big theatre, and some pillars with Corinthian capitals which rise up out of the confusion of alleys in the old city and are called Bacchus colonnades certainly belonged to a temple. The most impressive monument of Roman Laodicea which remains is the tetrapylon *(Page 97)*. Modern buildings also clustered round this structure, but they have been pulled down. Excavations in 1952 exposed the lower part of it, and a park round it now provides a view of this interesting monument. It appears to have been built in the reign of Emperor Septimius Severus, about 200 A.D., and once marked the place where the main street and an important side street crossed. As a result of the activities of the Directorate-General for Ancient Monuments and Museums of the Syrian Arab Republic, this harbour city has again been provided with a worthy monument of its great past.

GABALA (DJEBLE)

The little town of Djeble lies about 20 km south of Latakia, on the Mediterranean coast. It existed as a harbour in ancient oriental times and was for a time under the rule of the kings of Ugarit. We can probably identify Djeble as Gabala, a name which appears in Ugarit texts of the 14th and 13th centuries B.C. Of all the buildings from the period of pre-Islamic Gabala—the name Gabala can be traced back to scriptures of ancient writers—there remains only the big theatre *(Page 100)*. Apart from some unimportant remains, no other buildings of architectonic or historical significance have survived the centuries. The theatre, which was built during Roman times, is a remarkable structure since it was erected without the natural advantage of a sloping terrain.

The Directorate-General for Ancient Monuments and Museums has paid special attention to this interesting structure and has conducted excavations and restoration work since 1950.

PALMYRA

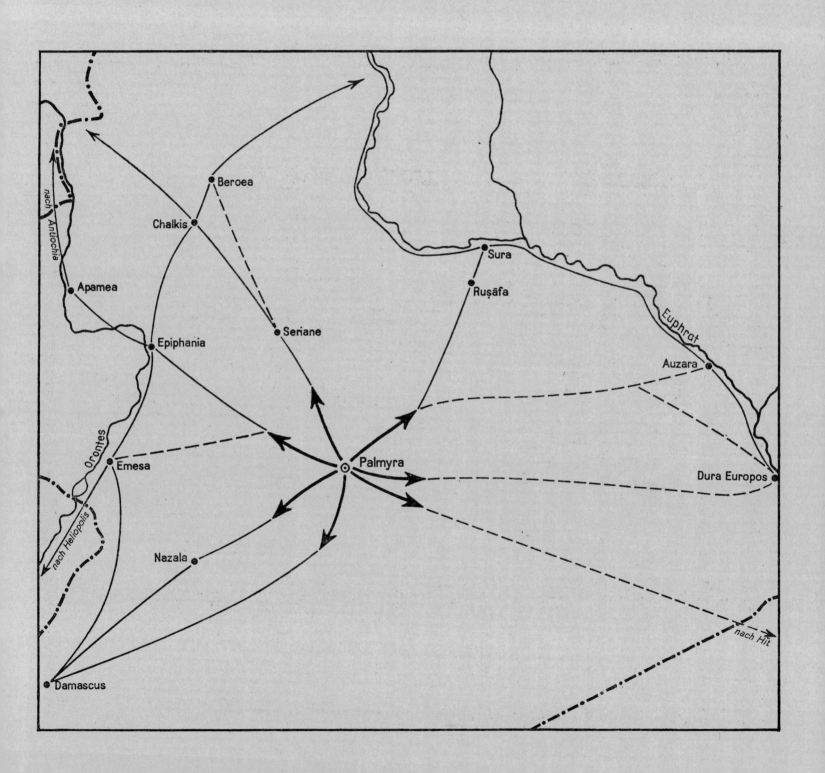

PALMYRA. *The gardens are surrounded by mud walls. There are no houses in these gardens, because the irrigated soil is too valuable.*

PALMYRA. *Date palms along the wall round the Efqa spring. In the background, some of the tower tombs of the western necropolis.*

PALMYRA. *This aerial photograph gives a good impression of the lay-out of the temple of Bel and its immediate surroundings. Taken from the southeast it shows—in the foreground, right— the remains of dwelling-houses of the 3rd century; above, the road which today crosses the ruined area on its way from Tadmur to Homs in Central Syria. The so-called triumphal arch and the big colonnaded street can be seen in the background. The temple site consists of the terrace with the outer wall, the porticoes of the courtyard and the temple of Bel itself.*

PALMYRA. *The south wall of the temple of Bel, seen from the gardens. In the course of time parts of the wall have begun to lean over somewhat. The front is divided by gabled windows and pilasters with Corinthian capitals; the windows were walled up when the building was turned into a fortress. The ancient pillar drums used again can be clearly detected.*

PALMYRA. *Portraits of (a) Wahballat and (b) his mother the Queen Regent Zenobia (until 272) have come down to us on coins like the bronze pieces shown here, which were minted in Alexandria. These are idealised portraits of the two rulers of Palmyra. Berlin, Coin Collection.*

PALMYRA. *View of the temple towards the south-west corner of the courtyard. The sides of the terrace on which the temple stands are over 200 m long. The Corinthian pillars of the colonnades are of varying height; some of them still bear the remains of the entablature. Many of the pillars are no longer standing; the drums lie around in the great temple courtyard or were used later as building material. The pillar drum in the foreground reveals the way in which the single drums were joined together by means of metal pegs in the four openings which were then sealed with lead.*

PALMYRA. *Courtyard of the temple of Bel. View to the northwest of the Arab fortress Qal'at ibn Ma'an towering above the ruins in the background. Right, part of the colonnade and the wall round the temple.*

PALMYRA. *The pillars of the porticoes, on profiled bases, bear Corinthian capitals on which parts of the richly ornamented entablature have survived. In the background the cella.*

PALMYRA. *A path from outside leads up to the level of the temple terrace through an arched gateway; some steps make it possible to reach the courtyard without following the path to the end. Sacrificial processions approached the altar on this path and the house in which sacrificial feasts took place. The animals were also led up here. These buildings date back to the 1st century.*

PALMYRA. *The oasis gardens stretch right up to the temple of Bel. Part of the surrounding wall and of the porticoes of the inner courtyard are shown here. Dates, pomegranates and olives ripen in the gardens which are surrounded by mud walls.*

PALMYRA. *The temple proper of Bel seen from the east. On this side the peristyle, the pillar-lined path surrounding the temple, is still well preserved. The capitals are missing; they were bronze and were therefore stolen. The pinnacles found near the temple were probably at the edge* *of the temple roof and have been put back there; these were an element taken over from ancient oriental architecture. The cella has a number of gabled windows, and pilasters and half-pillars with Corinthian and Ionic (volute) capitals on the shorter sides.* PALMYRA. *Part of the peristyle of the temple of Bel, with its pillars robbed of their capitals.*

PALMYRA. *View of the wall surrounding the temple of Bel from the outside. It was turned into a fortress wall in Islamic Arab times with the windows being walled up and many parts of the ancient structure being used again. In the background, the Corinthian pillars of the colonnade in the temple courtyard.*

PALMYRA. *Relief at the entrance to the temple of Bel; stemming from the architrave of the peristyle. In the upper part, left—not well preserved—a battle between a warrior standing on a war chariot and a legendary snake-footed animal. Right, behind the warrior, gods who are clearly helping him. Under an egg and dart a relief of a vine on which the remains of the original painting can still be seen.*

PALMYRA. *The great temple portal is encircled by several bands of ornamentation which, together with those on the triumphal arch, are certainly amongst the most beautiful work of this kind in Palmyra.*

PALMYRA. *The ceilings of the niches in the temple of Bel are richly ornamented. On the ceiling of the south niche, where the statue of Bel, the main god, stood there is a rosette of various leaves between geometrical patterns.*

PALMYRA. *In the north niche of the temple of Bel stood the statues of the three gods of Palmyra, Bel, Jarhibol and Aglibol.*

PALMYRA. *Relief from the entablature of the temple of Bel, section: veiled women walk in solemn procession behind a camel which bears a cult object (no longer visible in the picture) on its back—a sacred stone (bactyl). The figures of the women are especially impressive because of their carriage and the flowing lines of their long robes.*

136

PALMYRA. *In the temple of Baalshamin the main god, Bel, was worshipped in his capacity as ruler of heaven and lord of rain, wind, thunder and lightning. The temple had a courtyard with a pillared hall.*

PALMYRA. *There was an altar in front of the temple of Baalshamin—seen here from the front—which bore an inscription in Greek and Palmyrean dated 115 A.D. Thus like the 1st century temenos it is older than the temple still standing and probably belonged to an older building. Investigations by an expedition from Switzerland under P. Collart in 1954–1956 revealed that there was in fact such a building.*

PALMYRA. *The pillars of the pronaos of the temple of Baalshamin bear consoles on which statues were set up. The inscription on the bearing stone shown here mentions the building of the temple in 130 A.D. by Male, son of Jarhai.*

PALMYRA. The temple of Baalshamin, seen from the east. The cella is a rectangular building with a window in each of the longer sides. It could be entered through the pronaos, whose pillars bear Corinthian capitals and consoles. The temple was surrounded by a pillared courtyard, of which there are still some remains.

PALMYRA. Back view of the temple of Baalshamin showing the way in which the façade was divided up by pilasters with Corinthian capitals.

PALMYRA. *The triumphal arch, built about 200 A.D., spanned with its three gateways the broad carriage road and the covered paths on either side. Through the gate, to the northwest, the ruins of the Arab fortress.*

PALMYRA. *The triumphal arch on the long pillared street is richly ornamented with high reliefs standing out from the stone.*

PALMYRA. *The long main street of Palmyra with its Corinthian pillars still bearing part of the entablature makes a striking impression on all who see it. We look down the street towards the triumphal arch, whence it continues, curving slightly, to the temple of Bel.*

PALMYRA. *View of the colonnade with its unchamfered pillars; consoles are set on the shafts. Including base and capital, the pillars are nearly 10 m in height and still bear the lower parts of the entablature. In the background to the right, the tetrapylon.*

PALMYRA. *The pillars which rested on the lower pillars of the great colonnade and supported the roof of an upper gallery have survived.*

PALMYRA. *The theatre is close behind the pillared street, not far from the tetrapylon which marked the centre of the city. In the far background, on the hill, the ruins of the Arab fortress Qal'at ibn Ma'an.*

PALMYRA. *Architectural fragments which once had a place high up on arches or on the entablature now lie in the sand.*

PALMYRA. *The Corinthian columns are very well preserved on a number of pillars in the main street, like the one shown here. The rectangular holes in the shaft served to anchor the consoles.*

PALMYRA. *Everywhere amongst the ruins the visitor meets with decorative architectural elements. This bust emerging from a wreath decorated the keystone of a gateway arch in the big colonnade.*

148

PALMYRA. Arches topped the gateways leading from the great pillared street into side streets or important public buildings. These arches were often decorated in their upper parts by a keystone with a relief.

PALMYRA. Console with a richly decorated profile and a wreath on its front side. The statue of a very important personality stood on it. Despite the large number of pillars with consoles for statues, practically no examples of Palmyrean statuary have been discovered, not even in fragments. This gives rise to the assumption—supported by the evidence of an inscription—that the statues were all of bronze and were later melted down and thus disappeared, like the valuable jewellery from the graves which fell into the hands of robbers.

149

PALMYRA. *The row of pillars on the main street is interspersed with arched gateways, their archivolts resting on pilasters.*

PALMYRA. *The ruins at the great colonnade. Left, in the background, a pillar of honour and the palm gardens of Tadmur. The mountains are part of the ranges which stretch from the Euphrates right across the Syrian desert to the neighbourhood of Damascus. Near Palmyra they reach heights between 550 m (Qal'at ibn Ma'an) and 900 m. In spring the entire area of the ruins and the surrounding desert is carpeted with flowering grass, weeds and flowers. Herds of sheep wander through the former metropolis, but vegetation dries up quickly in the summer sun.*

PALMYRA. *The front of the stage (see Page 154) was also divided up architectonically on the side façade; above the side door to the stage are a semi-circular niche and a gabled niche.*

PALMYRA. *The little theatre of Palmyra has been completely excavated. A view into the semi-circular auditorium from one of the two entrances to the orchestra, carefully paved with rectangular stones. Thirteen rows of seats in the lower tier have survived. They are divided by steps into eleven sections. The main entrance for spectators was in the middle. In the background, the oasis gardens.*

PALMYRA. *View of the stage and the stage front of the theatre. Including the stage building, the stage measured 10.5 m in depth and 48 m in length. The stage front is relieved by three exedra of which the central one had four high pillars supporting an architrave.*

PALMYRA. *Syrian excavations under A. Bounni have exposed the temple of the god Nabo. From the entrance to the temenos we see the courtyard in which the altar stands and the cella of the temple, of which the terrace and the remains of pillars have survived. In the background, part of the big colonnade.*

PALMYRA. *There is a structure which was probably an altar in front of the entrance to the cella of the temple of Nabo; it is in the form of a small temple surrounded by pillars.*

PALMYRA. *A relief of the goddess Ashtar—the Babylonian Ishtar—was found in 1966 during excavations in the area of the temple of Nabo. Damascus, National Museum.*

PALMYRA. Section of a mosaic depicting the god of health, Asklepios or Aesculapius, holding a staff with a snake twined round it in one hand. This symbol was already known in ancient oriental times and has survived as the sign of the doctor right down to our own time. Museum of Palmyra.

PALMYRA. To the east of the temple of Bel excavations have exposed 3rd century dwelling-houses, where a number of mosaics were found.

PALMYRA. The agora, the place where citizens assembled, handed down to us in its present form from the 2nd century, was surrounded by colonnades. Speakers addressed the crowd from a low platform. Eleven entrances ensured that a large number of people could enter or leave the place quickly. In the background, the pillared street.

PALMYRA. The tetrapylon stands where the main street crossed an important side street. In practice it marked the centre of the city. Four granite Corinthian pillars, bearing a richly ornamented entablature, rise up on four socles made of huge square stones which rest on a platform 18 m in length. Between the pillars, on each socle, stood a statue.

PALMYRA. The tetrapylon was reconstructed after 1963 by the Directorate-General for Ancient Monuments and Museums. The original pillars of rose granite were probably brought from the Assuan region in Upper Egypt. View of the great colonnade.

PALMYRA. *The so-called Camp of Diocletian investigated by the Polish expedition lies at the foot of a hill from which there is a good view over the entire ruined area. In the background to the left, the great colonnade, to the right, the temple of Bel.*

PALMYRA. *Pillar of honour between the temple of Bel and the Efqa spring. It was set up again in 1964 by the Syrian Ancient Monuments administration. It was originally erected in 139 A.D. —the year 450 of the Seleucid era according to which dates were calculated in Palmyra—by the Senate and population in honour of Bariki and Moqimo, prominent citizens.*

PALMYRA. *Near the northwest end of the great colonnade stands the so-called burial temple, a house-tomb of the 3rd century. The pillars and part of the portico gable have survived. The Syrian Ancient Monuments Administration is doing restoration work here. In the background, the ruins of Qal'at ibn Ma'an.*

PALMYRA. *In the foreground, the Camp of Diocletian, in the background the temple of Bel and the gardens of Tadmur, which stand out dark against the yellowish-brown surroundings. Behind, the salt fields which enabled the inhabitants of Palmyra to extract their own salt in ancient times.*

PALMYRA. *Mausoleum of Arlius Marona, built in 236 A.D., according to a foundation inscription. The partially restored walls of the building are still standing and clearly show the temple-like form of such a grave. It resembles a cella and had pillars surrounding it—now vanished. Later on the building no longer served its original purpose and was turned into a dwelling-house. A relief discovered in it depicts a Palmyrean merchant and his ship.*

PALMYRA. *Bust relief from a grave, showing a couple whose names are given in the Palmyrean inscription on the relief. Damascus, National Museum.*

PALMYRA. *Tower tomb of Kithot in the Valley of the Graves in the western necropolis. Kithot, son of Taimarso, built the grave in 40 A.D. In the upper part of the tower, about 10 m above the ground, there is a relief of a burial feast, the oldest of its kind yet found in Palmyra. Behind the dead man, who is resting on a couch, stand three members of his family—his wife and two sons—and a slave. Their names are given in the Palmyrean inscription. The arch above the scene is ornamented with vines.*

PALMYRA. *Among the tower tombs, on a hill slope, the grave of Jamblikhos (Jamliku) stands out because of its size, its decorations and its good state of preservation. It was built in 83 A.D.*

PALMYRA. *Tower tomb of Elakhbel in the Valley of the Graves, built in 103 A.D. The building consists of five storeys. On the third storey, on the outside, there is a relief in an arched niche showing a sarcophagus between two pilasters.*

PALMYRA. *This overturned gable with rich leaf decorations and a rosette in the middle lies in the Valley of the Graves. It indicates the importance which the inhabitants of Palmyra attached to a worthy burial of their dead.*

165

PALMYRA. *The dead were buried in these graves —loculi cubicula—which were cut into the rocky ground horizontally from a passage-way or built into tower tombs. Here there were three graves one above the other. The loculi were generally closed by a stone slab showing high relief portraits of the dead person.*

PALMYRA. *Wall paintings from the Grave of the Three Brothers in the southwest necropolis. These frescoes painted on chalk on the south wall of the east passage-way about the 2nd half of the 2nd century depict animals—far below and hardly visible here. Above, rectangles standing on their corners with rhombuses inside them, further winged figures supporting medallions with pictures of men and women. Left, the figure of a woman with a child. The vaults were also painted, to suggest architecture. Traces of six loculi one above the other can still be seen.*

166

The traveller arriving at Palmyra after the long journey through the desert from Damascus or from Homs in Central Syria can scarcely believe his eyes when he sees this oasis with its magnificent monuments in the midst of the solitary desert. These ancient ruins, certainly the most impressive in the Near East, are about 400 m above sea level, at the foot of the long range of chalk hills stretching from the Euphrates almost as far as Damascus. One of these hills is crowned by an Arab fortress, Qual'at ibn Ma'an. A broad view of the desert opens up from here *(Page 121)* and a few white saltworks shimmer on the horizon. The ruins below the fortress cover an area of about 6 square kilometres and, to the south of them, green gardens stand out against their yellowish-brown surroundings. To the east shine the houses of Tadmur, which is beginning to be what Palmyra once was—the centre of the Syrian desert.

PALMYRA'S PLACE IN HISTORY

Palmyra—or Tadmur, as it was called in the days before and after antiquity—is situated about halfway between the Euphrates, the great traffic route of eastern Hither Asia, and the Mediterranean coast with its many harbours. The caravan route from the Euphrates through Tadmur to the cultivated part of Syria and on to the coast or to Egypt and Palestine was already used by merchants with their pack-asses in ancient oriental times. Often enough the merchants were followed by the armies of the Mesopotamian kings. A number of ground-water oases following the mountain chain which cuts across the Syrian desert provided travellers with the necessary drinking water. As trade increased between the Near Eastern countries and more distant lands like India, a number of new routes were opened up which passed through Palmyra. In Roman times Palmyra was the centre and junction of a network of routes covering the northern part of the Syrian-Arab desert. Many of these were mere tracks not always open to traffic, especially during the rains, but some paved roads were built by the Romans and the course of these can still be detected, especially from the air.

The advent of the camel, which needed little water, moved faster than the ass and could transport bigger loads, was also important for the rise of Palmyra. Where it had hitherto been impossible to travel because of the long distances between watering-places—or at any rate only with the help of large quantities of water carried in leather bags—camel caravans could now travel without difficulty. Trade provided Palmyra with the foundations of its wealth, but other factors favourable to a desert economy should also be remembered. Palmyra had a hinterland; a number of more or less permanently inhabited villages whose inhabitants were engaged partly in arable farming and partly in animal husbandry—a fact for which there is archaeological evidence for the Roman period. After the winter rains the desert literally blossoms overnight, producing a wealth of grasses and herbs which provided nomads and villagers with plentiful grazing. Grain was also grown there at that time, and after the harvest some of the desert population moved towards the more civilised part of the country. Bushes and isolated trees such as the terebintha certainly grew in the region north of Palmyra, known as Palmyrene, in ancient times. Thus in addition to dried dung also firewood for cooking and for heating purposes during the cold winter months was available. After people had learned to dig deeper wells, in the early 1st millennium B.C., it was possible to supply the settlements round Palmyra with ground water, in addition to the rainwater collected in cisterns. The country west of Palmyra was also more densely populated in ancient times than it is now, and under the protection of the Roman Empire farming went on from the regularly cultivated region far into the Syrian desert. Southwest of Palmyra, where a great Caliph's palace was built in the 8th century (Qasr el-Kher el-Gharbi), there was a flourishing oasis artificially supplied with water which belonged to Palmyra. The city was thus not so isolated as it appears today.

Palmyra itself proved very suitable for permanent settlement because of the natural conditions prevailing there. The Efqa spring *(Pages 119, 120)* sends up about 150 litres per second of sulphurous water from a grotto over 100 m in length. The water is still channelled into a network of canals which water the surrounding desert and date palms, pomegranates and olive trees flourish in the gardens *(Page 120)*. People paid for the use of water from the Efqa spring, just as they do today. Another spring—the "sweet" or "seraglio" spring—provided drinking water which was brought to the city through a pipe from a wadi about 10 km to the northwest; the water was collected by means of a groundwater system (foggara). The saltworks were probably also not unimportant for the supply of Palmyra; these lie to the south and east of the town. When the rainwater dried out here at the end of spring, the salt which the water dissolved out of the soil settled and could be used by the inhabitants of Palmyra and the nomads of the surrounding region.

In view of all this it is understandable that Palmyra should have been so long inhabited and was able to rise to a position of great importance. The French archaeologist R. du Mesnil du Buisson brought to light near the Efqa springs the remains of a structure dating back to the later Stone Age. Excavations by the same scholar in the courtyard of the big temple of Bel produced evidence that Palmyra was permanently inhabited in the early Bronze Age, about 2000 B.C., and also in the later Bronze Age (1600–1200 B.C.). The inhabitants were probably in the main members of Amorite West Semitic tribes who, also at about this time, began to penetrate into the neighbouring civilised Syrian and Mesopotamian region from the North Syrian desert. The first written information about Palmyra, which was already called Tadmer—Tadmur—at that time, can be found in cuneiform inscriptions of the early 2nd millennium B.C. They describe Palmyra as a place on the trade routes of that time which also had to defend itself against attacks by predatory nomad tribes. At the end of the 2nd millennium the Assyrian king Tiglath-pileser I (1112–1074) pursued Aramaic tribes as far as Tadmur.

Over a long period thereafter there are no inscriptions mentioning Palmyra and when information again appears in the 1st century B.C. it is mentioned as an important city. It must have begun to flourish in the Hellenic period, and an inscription dated 44 B.C. shows that there was already a temple of Bel—the old Syrian Baal—in Palmyra.

Palmyra was at first not included in the Roman province of Syria set up in 63 B.C. and it managed to survive independently between the Romans and the Parthians, but it must have been occupied by the Romans in the early 1st century. From that time onwards it played an important role on the frontier between the Roman Empire and the Parthians. Palmyrean archers had a good reputation in the Roman army. The Roman Emperor Hadrian made Palmyra a free city in 129 A.D. and his name is sometimes added to it in recognition of his favour.

Tribal order still influenced the organisation of the city and the nomad order survived after its inhabitants had settled down. A number of inscriptions indicate that Palmyra was governed by a city council, which later became the Senate. The Roman Empire was represented both by a garrison and by a high official who also collected the taxes. Septimius Severus (193–211) raised Palmyra to the status of a Roman colony and it was included in his day in the Province of Syria Phoenice, whose capital was Emesa (Homs). This not only gave Palmyra higher prestige; its inhabitants now had Italian rights and were not required to pay land taxes. The granting of this favour by the Roman Emperors, some of whom visited the city, can be explained to a very great extent by Palmyra's importance in the conflict between the Romans and the Parthians. This emerged clearly when disturbances broke out in the Empire after the death of Septimius Severus; these were exploited by its neighbours, including the Persian Sassanids in the east who had taken the place of the Parthians. The Palmyrean Odainat owed his rise to this difficult situation for the Romans.

A period of increasing political power for the economically prosperous Palmyra—the period of the princes of Palmyra (c. 235–273)—began with the advent of Odainat (Odenathus). As a Roman general Odainat, who was first Senator and then Consul in Palmyra, succeeded in winning a victory over the invading Persians. He was then given the title of *corrector* of the entire Orient by the Emperor Gallienus. He did the Imperial house a further service by defeating a rival Roman Emperor on the Orontes. Odainat was well aware of his power. He behaved like a Roman Emperor and was even called "king of kings" in an inscription on a statue; this was the old Oriental rulers' title. He also succeeded in winning other campaigns against the Persians and advanced as far as the Sassanid capital Ctesiphon on the Tigris (near present-day Baghdad). Odainat was murdered in 267 in Emesa, under circumstances which have never been revealed, and since his eldest son was also killed at the same time, his younger son Wahballat succeeded him. Wahballat took his father's titles, including the high-sounding "king of kings", but was too young to govern by himself, so that his mother Zenobia ruled in his stead. The most brilliant and also the final golden age of Palmyra now began *(Page 123)*.

As its name indicates, the dynasty came from the Arab population of Palmyra. Aramaic-speaking Arabs had for a long time lived in Palmyra and inter-mingled with the older, also Semitic, population. A special form developed out of the Aramaic script of which there is evidence from about the first century B.C. A large number of such Palmyrean inscriptions date from the time of the princes of Palmyra. The language of these texts is an

PALMYRA. *Plan of the city, with the help of the plan of Palmyra shown in: K. Michalowski, Palmyra (Warszawa 1968).*

1 *Efqa spring*
2 *Seraglio spring*
3 *Temple of Bel*
4 *Temple of Nabo*
5 *Temple of Baalshamin*
6 *Triumphal arch*
7 *Great colonnade*
8 *Theatre*
9 *Agora*
10 *Hall for sacrificial feasts*
11 *Tetrapylon*
12 *Burial temple*
13 *Flag temple, Camp of Diocletian*
14 *Pillars of honour*
15 *3rd century houses*
16 *Basilica*
17 *Mausoleum of the Maronas*
18 *Grave of Jamblikhos*
19 *Museum of Palmyra*

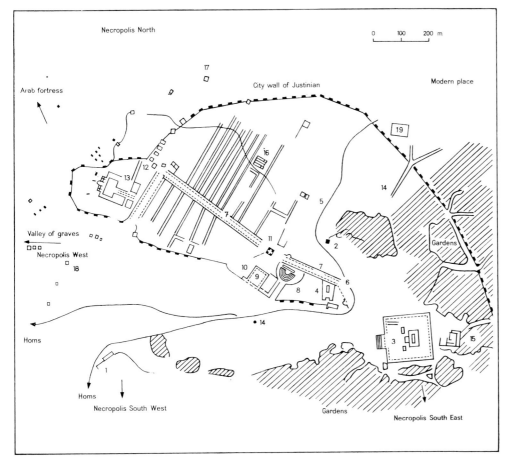

Aramaic which in its spoken form was strongly influenced by Arabic. Greek was also spoken and written in Palmyra. This emerges especially clearly from the so-called "tariff of Palmyra", which was carved on a stone slab 5 m wide in Greek and Palmyrean script and languages, in 137 A.D. This inscription of more than 400 lines consists of a Senate decree on tariffs, including regulations on fees for the use of the two springs in the city. It was discovered near the agora, the assembly place of Palmyra.

In this and other inscriptions and in numerous smaller finds in the city, the role of Palmyra in ancient trade can be clearly seen. The city enjoyed special prosperity after the kingdom of the Nabataeans, with its capital Petra, was incorporated in the Roman Empire under Trajan and it was able to take over some of Petra's trade. Palmyra was not only a meeting-place for foreign merchants; it also took an active part in long-distance trade. Luxury goods, even including Chinese silks and Indian spices, took first place in this trade. A relief from Palmyra shows a merchant standing proudly beside his ship which evidently sailed the Persian Gulf, and there is evidence of Palmyrean trading in many places, including Kharax (the modern Basra), Vologesias (near Seleucia on the Tigris), Dura Europos and clearly, too, in Coptos in Upper Egypt.

Wahballat and the Queen Regent Zenobia, whose Aramaic name was Batzabbai, were able to take advantage of Palmyra's role as middleman when they proceeded to extend its influence in the political and military field. A campaign against Egypt began under General Zabdas at the end of 271. It was successful and was followed by an advance into

Asia Minor. A large part of the Eastern Roman Empire came under Palmyra's control. Coins with the image of Wahballat or his mother Zenobia were also minted in Alexandria in Egypt. The Roman Emperor Aurelian took his army by forced marches into Asia Minor and Syria, defeated Zenobia near Antioch and Emesa and pursued her back to the walls of Palmyra. Zenobia, who hoped for help from the Persians and from neighbouring Bedouin tribes, retreated into her capital and refused to surrender. Aurelian then cut off the Persian relief forces and succeeded in persuading the Arab and Aramaic tribes around Palmyra to remain neutral. When Zenobia realised that her position was hopeless she tried to escape to the Euphrates on a dromedary and get Persian help there herself, but Roman cavalry caught up with her at the river and took her captive. Palmyra now opened its gates to the Roman Emperor, who entered the city in the autumn of 272. The treasury was confiscated and sent to Emesa. A few prominent citizens were deported, including Queen Zenobia. There is conflicting evidence about Zenobia's subsequent fate, but it appears that she died near Rome.

The city of Palmyra rebelled soon after the withdrawal of the main body of Roman troops and massacred the garrison of six hundred archers. Aurelian returned when he received this news; no mercy was shown this time and the city was taken without battle, plundered and set on fire. Palmyra never recovered from this disaster. Its downfall was followed by increasingly frequent Bedouin attacks on caravans and the Sassanids succeeded in establishing their position again on the Euphrates. Under the Emperor Diocle-

tian (284–305) the Romans built a limes with forts right across the Syrian desert as far as Palmyra, and trade, which shifted to other routes, suffered under these conditions. The city fell into decline, only reviving somewhat under the Eastern Roman Emperor Justinian I (527–565), when a new city wall was built and it was well supplied with water and used as a base against the Arab tribes of the Syrian desert. But it never regained its erstwhile importance.

In 634 Islamic Arab troops under the General Khalid ibn al-Walid entered Palmyra-Tadmur. It was built up as a fortress and also used as a market-place, the temple of Baal was turned into a citadel. But it did not again play an important role. Under Osman-Turkish rule it was forgotten and fell into ruins. The last news of its former splendour reached Europe through Benjamin of Tudela who visited Palmyra in 1172.

REDISCOVERY

There was news of Palmyra again only in the 17th century, when it was visited by the Italian Pietro della Valle in 1616 and 1625, by the Frenchman Jean-Baptiste Tavernier in 1630 and by a group of English merchants in 1678 who reached Tadmur from Aleppo. Although the latter fared badly—they were captured by Bedouins and only released on payment of a large ransom—they returned there later on. Pastor Halifax, who accompanied them, brought back to Europe the first copies of Palmyrean inscriptions. In 1751 two Englishmen, H. Dawkins and R. Wood, visited Tadmur and made drawings of the ruins, copied inscriptions and published the results of their investigations in a book "Les

Ruines de Palmyre", in 1753. This work not only provided the basis for de-coding Palmyrean inscriptions but also drew attention to Syrian ruins. The place was frequently visited by travellers in the 19th century with the inscriptions attracting special attention. The longest text, the so-called "tariff of Palmyra", was discovered in 1881.

Expeditions from various countries took part in the archaeological and restoration work done in Palmyra since the beginning of the 20th century and the Directorate-General for Ancient Monuments and Museums of the Syrian Arab Republic has taken an increasingly active part. In 1902 and 1917 German research work under T. Wiegand was conducted in Palmyra and the most important monuments were photographed and described. During the mandatory period it was mainly French scholars who worked here. In 1929 H. Seyrig, at that time Director of the *"Antikendienst"* in Beirut, arranged for the small Arab settlement inside the Temple of Bel to move to the area northeast of the ruins, where present-day Tadmur began to grow up. Extensive restoration work was done and up to the Second World War French, German and Danish experts conducted excavations in Palmyra. After the war archaeological research by the Syrian Ancient Monuments Administration concentrated on the little theatre of Palmyra and some graves. A Swiss mission under P. Collart investigated buildings built previous to the Baalshamin temple from 1954 to 1956, and a group of Polish archaeologists under K. Michałowski conducted excavations in the area of the so-called Camp of Diocletian, in the northwest part of the ruins. The Syrians re-constructed the tetrapylon and the burial

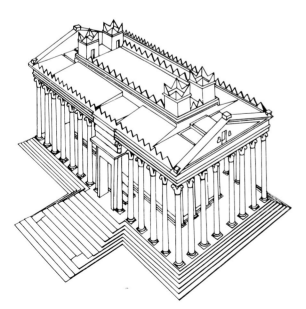

PALMYRA. *Reconstruction of the temple of Bel after R. Amy, Syria 27 (1950), Fig. 17.*

temple, and in 1963–1965 A. Bounni continued work begun by the Wiegand expedition on a temple site, where he has achieved notable results. The site turned out to be that of a temple of the god Nabo.

Thus archaeologists and philologists of the Syrian Arab Republic and a number of other countries have worked together in Palmyra to investigate this gem of Syria's past, to preserve its monuments and to provide new centres of interest through their excavations. A walk through these ruins in the heart of the Syrian desert becomes more and more interesting as time goes on.

A WALK THROUGH THE RUINS

Let us start with Palmyra's sacred places, the temples of the gods Bel, Baalshamin and Nabo. The merging of several traditions can be seen especially clearly in Palmyra's religion. It is in most cases extremely difficult to find an ethnic explanation or to localise the origin of the more than sixty deities known from inscriptions or pictures found in Palmyra. Along with ancient Semitic gods, including the main gods Bel or Baal and Baalshamin, there are gods of Arab origin—the most important being Allat. Some Greek and Roman gods were also among them and the deification of Roman Emperors also left traces in Palmyra. At the head of the pantheon stands a trinity—Bel, Jarhibol (sun god) and Aglibol (moon god). Baalshamin, the ruler of heaven, embodied Bel as lord of the rain which gave the earth fertility. Another god, Malakbel, was often revered as god of the sun, like Jarhibol; that is why he was sometimes called Shamash, like the sun god of the Babylonians. The Syrian

goddess Atargatis, whose temple was excavated at Dura Europos, and the Babylonian god Nabu or Nabo should also be mentioned. It has been known for some years that this god had his own temple at Palmyra. An anonymous "good and merciful" god, to whom many inscriptions at the Efqa spring were dedicated, was much revered from the 2nd century A.D. onwards. The Efqa spring was the ancient cultic centre.

The temple of Bel is without doubt the most important monument at Palmyra; here the trinity—Bel (Baal, also Bol in Palmyrean), Jarhibol and Aglibol—were worshipped. The temple is situated at the edge of the oasis gardens in the southern part of the city *(Pages 122, 124–137).* The two biggest sections of it are the large, almost square sacred area (Temenos) and the temple itself, which stands on a substructure *(Pages 126, 128).* The temple was built on an artificial hill formed by throwing up earth over the ruins of Bronze Age and Hellenic buildings. The entrance to the surrounding wall, decorated with Corinthian pillars and interspersed with rectangular gabled windows, was on the west side *(Page 130).* It is concealed today by the bastion of the Islamic Arab citadel which turned the surrounding wall into a closed fortress wall and made use of many elements of the ancient structure, especially the pillar drums *(Page 122).* The big paved courtyard is surrounded by a portico with Corinthian pillars *(Pages 124, 125).* To the left of the entrance a ramp leads up to the level of the temple courtyard from the outside and ends in a sacrificial altar beside which there are also the remains of a house where sacrificial meals were eaten *(Page 125).* Farther to the south, in the courtyard, there is a large sacred pool which served for cultic cleansings. The temple itself *(Page 126)*, whose richly ornamented portal *(Page 131)* faces the entrance to the courtyard, is a rectangular naos with a peristyle, only partly preserved, the pillars of which were crowned by bronzed capitals *(Pages 128, 129)*. Some reliefs, now set up near the temple entrance, come from the entablature of the peristyle *(Pages 132, 135, 137)*. Niches can be seen on the northern and southern sides of the cella in which stood figures of the gods. Bel, Jarhibol and Aglibol were revered in the north *(Page 136)* and Bel alone in the south niche; the ceilings of the niches were richly decorated *(Page 136)*. These niches, like the temple as a whole, show that the building was Syrian-Oriental. A Christian church was set up in the cella in Byzantine times (5th to 6th centuries) and later on, until 1929, there was a mosque here. This main temple of Palmyra was built in the 1st and 2nd centuries A.D., as inscriptions show. The written sources also reveal that there were earlier buildings here, too.

Not far from the present-day Hotel "Zenobia" lies another and especially well preserved temple, the temple of Baalshamin *(Pages 138, 140, 141)*. A dedicatory inscription shows that this temple was built in 130 A.D. *(Page 140)*, but it is certain that another temple had already occupied this site. The Temenos, for example, numerous remains of whose pillars can still be seen, dates back to the 1st century A.D. *(Page 138)*. An inscription of the year 149, on the other hand, shows that a colonnade was added to the south side of the courtyard at this time. Up to about the middle of the 2nd century A.D. the cult of the "ruler of heaven" flourished. This temple

was also turned into a Christian church in the 5th century. In front of it there is an altar bearing Palmyrean and Greek inscriptions mentioning the year 115 *(Page 140)*. The pronaos of the temple has six Corinthian pillars, of which the four in front have consoles.

A third Palmyrean temple stands near the so-called triumphal arch of the great colonnade *(Page 139)*. Thanks to research work done by Syrian archaeologists headed by A. Bounni, we know that this was the temple of the god Nabo, worshipped in Mesopotamia as the son of Marduk, as the god of writing and wisdom and as secretary of the gods *(Page 156)*. The Greeks and Romans placed him on a level with Apollo and his name often appears beside that of Bel on the Palmyrean tesserae, the invitation seals to sacrificial feasts. A small relief from the temple area shows the Babylonian Ishtar *(Page 157)*. A monumental gate gave access to the temple courtyard, which was surrounded by covered colonnades and in which an altar stood in front of the entrance to the cella *(Page 156)*. Steps led up to the cella, which was on a terrace and surrounded by a peristyle with Corinthian pillars. This structure, which again shows clearly Oriental features, probably dates back to the first half of the 1st century A.D.

The big colonnade which lined the main street of Palmyra and the so-called triumphal arch are two other important and impressive monuments of old Palmyra *(Pages 142–150)*. The triumphal arch stands at a place where, approached from the temple, the main street curves and then continues in a somewhat more westerly direction towards the tetrapylon *(Page 144)*. The gateway, built about 200 A.D., is richly ornamented with reliefs *(Page 143)*. A triangular gable

PALMYRA. *The Trinity Baalshamin (centre), Aglibol and Malakbel. Paris, Louvre. After R. Dussaud, La pénétration des Arabes en Syrie avant l'Islam (Paris 1955), p. 97, Fig. 18.*

rose above the great central arch. The structure was restored in 1931 and in 1957–58 by R. Amy and the Syrian Ancient Monuments Administration. The great colonnaded street itself, which is more than a kilometre in length, was probably the main business street of ancient Palmyra. Under the wooden-roofed colonnades with their Corinthian pillars *(Page 148)* were the shops of the artisans and traders, which opened on to the sidewalk—six metres wide. Consoles have survived on the pillars, about halfway up the column and on these stood statues of prominent citizens, as can be seen from the inscriptions *(Page 146)*. The street itself was 11 m in width. A number of important public buildings faced on to this street: Diocletian's baths, the theatre with the agora and behind the Senate, a sacred spring and the like.

The theatre, which was built in the first half of the 2nd century A.D. and only rescued again in 1952 from the sand which had drifted over it after the fall of Palmyra, is favourably situated in the middle of the business centre of the city *(Page 155)*. This was not usual for a theatre, but it was possible in this case because the building is not very large. The *skene* is 48 m long, the orchestra has a diameter of 20 m. The semi-circular auditorium still has thirteen rows of seats, which were divided up into eleven sectors by steps *(Page 153)*. The front of the stage building is strongly divided *(Pages 152, 154)*. Excavations by the Directorate-General for Ancient Monuments and Museums exposed the gangways and threw light on the neighbouring buildings which belonged to the theatre *(Page 155)*.

The agora stood west of the theatre *(Page 159)*. It was investigated by H. Seyrig and M. Duru in 1939. It is a rectangular building measuring 71 by 48 m and is surrounded by porticoes whose pillars bore consoles with figures of generals, caravan leaders, high officials and senators. At the northern end two fountains cooled the air and a low platform shows from where speakers addressed meetings. Adjacent to the agora is a structure which may have been a banquetting hall where ritual sacrificial feasts were held. Guests, invited by means of *tesserae*, small fragments of pottery, lay on banks running along the walls. The Senate building, standing in a courtyard surrounded by pillars, was also adjacent to the agora.

If we follow the colonnaded street farther to the northwest, we come to the tetrapylon, which marks where the main street crosses an important side street *(Page 160)*. This was restored by the Syrian Ancient Monuments Administration after 1963. The road now curves slightly to the north and ends at a building listed as a burial temple, where Syrian restoration work has also been done *(Page 162)*. This is a house-tomb of the 3rd century A.D. of which the pillars of the outer hall and part of the gable have survived. On another street, lined by pillars, which branches off almost at a right angle at the end of the big colonnade and proceeds in a southwesterly direction, stands the so-called Camp of Diocletian which has been investigated by Polish archaeologists since 1959 *(Pages 161, 162)*. This structure, which resembles the palace of the Emperor Diocletian at Spalatum (Split, Yugoslavia), can be reached through Praetorians' Gate. One comes first upon a tetrapylon and then a big courtyard with the so-called flag temple and a small temple to the Arab god Allat. This Camp of Diocletian is enclosed on three sides

PALMYRA. *Grave of the Three Brothers. Ground Plan. After Kh. Assa'ad—O. Taha, Welcome to Palmyra (Damascus 1966), p. 69.*

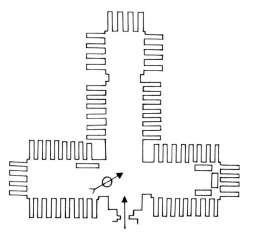

by part of the city wall which Justinian I caused to be built in the 6th century. Part of a wall was used here which dates back to the days of Zenobia and was destroyed by the troops of the Emperor Aurelian in 273. It had a total length of 12 km and surrounded Palmyra at that time. There were square towers built into the wall at intervals. A number of burial towers being suitable for defence were also included in Justinian's wall.

Of the dwellings in Palmyra little has so far been excavated. The ruins of 3rd century dwelling-houses are especially interesting, i.e. those of the golden age of Palmyra, to be found east of the temple of Bel (Page 158). Here the archaeologists H. Seyrig and M. Du-ru found a number of mosaics (Page 158). The pillars erected by the Senate in honour of prominent citizens (Page 161) are also worthy of mention.

Burials took place outside the city in necropoli in the north, west, southwest and southeast. The hard earth round Palmyra and the need to inter worthily the increasing number of dead resulting from the increase in population led to the use of more and more common graves instead of individual ones or house tombs. These were of two kinds: the underground grave (hypogeum) and the tower tomb. Nothing approaching all the graves around Palmyra have yet been discovered or investigated. Amongst the family graves—of which there is evidence from the 2nd century onwards—where some wealthy Palmyreans who had profited greatly by the beginning golden age found their last resting-places, those which deserve special mention are the burial temple and the mausoleum of the Marona family (Page 162, 163). Some of the underground burial places, most of which

were built in the 2nd and 3rd centuries, were when the Iraqi Oil Company was working discovered on the pipe-line. Amongst these hypogea the Grave of the Three Brothers in the southwest necropolis is certainly the best known; it is most worth seeing because of its ornamentation and size. A ramp leads down to the stone gate of the grave, over which Palmyrean inscriptions name the brothers Male, Sa'edi and Na'main as its builders in 140 A.D. Like other graves of its kind it has the form of an inverted capital T. All three gangways have grave shafts (loculi cubicula) driven horizontally into the rocks less than a metre apart—six each one above the other. Altogether, therefore, it was possible to bury 390 bodies here. Besides that there were also some sarcophagi decorated with sculptures, set up separately. The large number of burials possible indicates that this was a business undertaking; the builder and his heirs, who were also buried here, sold the other graves. The loculi were generally closed by stone slabs on which the portraits of the dead were chiselled in high relief (Pages 163, 166). Hundreds of these burial reliefs can be found in the museums of the world today. In a number of graves reliefs were discovered which show the dead reclining on couches at the burial feasts with their relatives. But the Grave of the Three Brothers is especially famous for its wall paintings, which are at the ends of the gangways and on the stucco which covers the brick vaults (Page 166). The Hellenistic style of painting reveals a strongly Oriental influence, also evident in the reliefs, especially in the strictly frontal aspect of the figures.

The burial towers may be regarded as typically Syrian; they are to be found in various

other places in Syria, for example on the middle reaches of the Euphrates and in the Hauran region. The most interesting of these in Palmyra are undoubtedly those in the western necropolis, in the so-called Valley of Graves. These are structures with a quadratic base above which there are several storeys with a large number of loculi; the storeys are linked by steps and often decorated with reliefs and paintings (cf. Page 164). Burial towers dating back to the 1st century A.D. have been found in Palmyra, the oldest of them connected with hypogea. Probably the best known are the towers of Kithot (Page 164) built in 40 A.D., the Jamblikhos or Jamliku (Page 164) built in 83 A.D. and the Elakhbel (Page 165) built in 103. Both the Directorate-General for Ancient Monuments and Museums and foreign expeditions have done good work in investigating and partially restoring the burial towers.

A large number of single finds, of which only the most important can be mentioned here, were rescued from the ruins at Palmyra—for example, the reliefs on the graves mentioned above, pictures of gods and prominent citizens, mosaics and objects of daily use. The desert climate has also been instrumental in preserving the garments of the dead in some burial towers, including silks which were probably imported from China. The most interesting finds are now in the museums of Damascus and Palmyra, but samples of Palmyrean culture and art can be seen in many other museums in the world. There are without doubt many more interesting monuments still hidden under the dunes and sand of the desert in and near Palmyra, waiting to be discovered.

THE EASTERN ROMAN BYZANTINE PERIOD

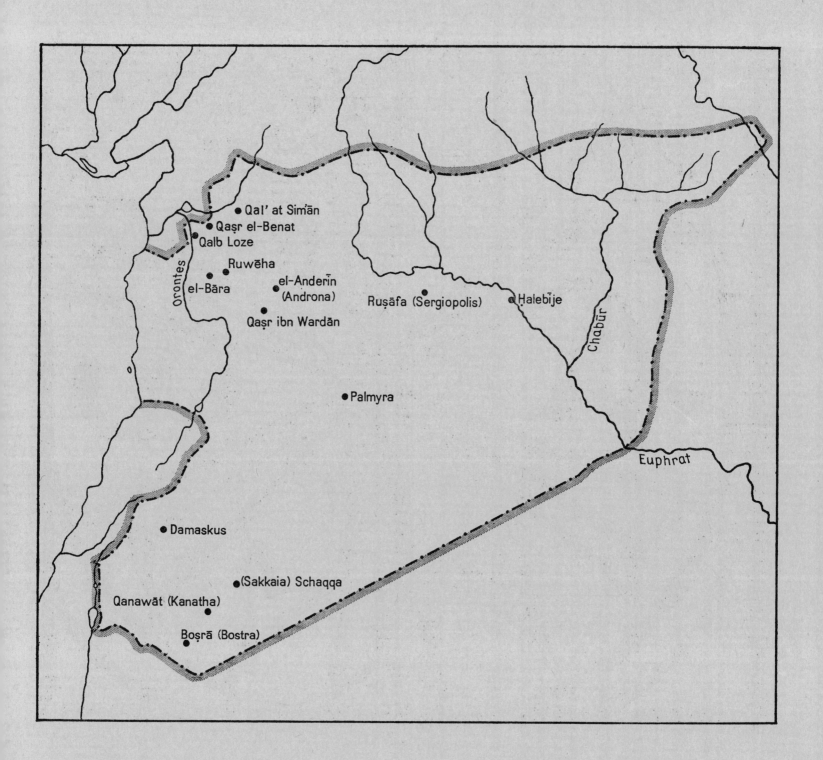

Qal' at Sim'ān

Qaṣr el-Benat

Qalb Loze

Ruwēha

el-Bāra

el-Anderīn
(Androna)

Ruṣāfa (Sergiopolis)

Ḥalebīje

Orontes

Chabūr

Qaṣr ibn Wardān

Palmyra

Euphrat

Damaskus

(Sakkaia) Schaqqa

Qanawāt (Kanatha)

Boṣrā (Bostra)

NEAR HAMA. *This mosaic floor, 2.81 by 2.85 m, still very well preserved, comes from a building of the Byzantine period. Within a border of plaited work there are birds amongst branches emerging from vases, and a Christian cross. Damascus, National Museum.*

SERGIOPOLIS (RUSAFA). *View from the west over the ruins, which are covered with tall grasses and wild grain in spring. There are many crater-like hollows here—evidence of collapsed mud buildings and private diggings. In the back-ground, left, Basilica B, and behind it the Basilica of Sergius, beside it a part of the city wall in which the arcades of the defence passage can be seen. Right, a later building.*

SERGIOPOLIS. *There have also been excavations in the region of the so-called Basilica B and some of the buildings to the southwest of the church have been investigated. The photograph shows a gate with a broadly profiled framework, built of the material mainly used at Rusafa, a white, translucent gypsum stone.*

SERGIOPOLIS. *The ruins of the Sergius basilica, still standing, which is the most important build-ing in Rusafa, make it possible to reconstruct approximately what it once looked like. The mid-dle aisle—F. Sarre's photograph shows it from the south side aisle—was first supported by three tremendous arches with a span of 10 m each and separated from the two side aisles. Smaller arches were then let into them which were supported by plain pillars with Byzantine capitals.*

SERGIOPOLIS. *The north gate was the most magnificently decorated gateway of the city. On the inner side, an arcade with six pillars stands against the city wall; it supports a reinforcement 1.2 m in thickness which here gives the crown of the city wall a breadth of about 4 m. The main* *gate in the middle has a richly profiled framework 60 cm in width and consoles decorated with acanthus leaves support the lintel, which has a rosette at the centre. The frames of the side gates have splendid profiles and archivolts. The photo shows the partially buried building.*

SERGIOPOLIS. *The plastic decoration of the ar-cades and the carefully designed capitals can be very clearly seen here. The pillars stand out 70 cm from the wall. Corinthian capitals support the arches of the arcades, the biggest of which, over the central gate, has a span of 4.7 m. The somewhat projecting sill which follows the arch (archivolt) is divided up into a number of bands of decoration—one a garland of vine leaves and grapes.*

SERGIOPOLIS. F. Sarre's photograph shows the main apse of the martyry, the memorial church to the martyr Sergius, taken from the east. The apse, divided by three tall round arches, is 8.3 m across. Only very little of the rich ornamentation remains. In the background, the city wall of Sergiopolis.

SERGIOPOLIS. The architectonic decoration of the side apses has survived the centuries better than that of the main apse. The archivolt with its bands of ornaments is 70 cm wide and rests on pilasters with acanthus capitals. The keystone of the archivolt, which has shifted slightly, shows a Greek cross framed in a wreath.

QAL'AT SIM'AN. The narthex of the south basilica is richly decorated. The pressure of the arches on the gateway is here taken up by columns, pilasters and pillars with acanthus-decorated capitals. The pillar capital is especially interesting; here acanthus leaves are carved in such a way as to suggest that they are wind-blown.

QAL'AT SIM'AN. *Seen from the south, from the main entrance to the monastery compound, the pilgrimage church is especially impressive. Since this was the side actually on view, a narthex —front hall—was added to the south basilica. Three big portals gave access to it. Its arches, with profiled frames, rest on pillars and pilasters. Behind it four doors lead into the church. In the foreground, the tracks of a railway used during restoration work.*

QAL'AT SIM'AN. *The baptistery, in the south part of the surrounding wall, is also an important monument of Byzantine-Christian architecture. It is a square building, its sides about 20 m in length, with a central room connected with a three-aisle basilica.*

SERGIOPOLIS. *The basilica of Sergius is still sufficiently well preserved to give a good impression of what it once looked like. View from the middle aisle with its arches on pillars bearing Byzantine capitals.*

184

QAL'AT SIM'AN. *The central building lies in the middle of the cross-shaped pilgrimage church. It may have been roofed by a dome. Its octagonal form is turned into something approaching a square by means of small apses. The apsidiole seen here is between the north and east basilica. Aerial photographs have revealed that not all four arms of the cross, the four basilicas, are at right angles to the central building.*

QAL'AT SIM'AN. *The wide arches of the octagon rest on columns and pillars with acanthus capitals, between them a richly ornamented console. Profile and bands of ornamentation of the archivolts can be clearly seen here.*

QAL'AT SIM'AN. *The central building, 27 m across, opens towards the four basilicas with high arches. The most important of these was the east basilica, which has a main apse and two side apses with arched windows.*

QAL'AT SIM'AN. *The pilgrimage church in spring, seen from the south. Its splendid situation and the wonderful view, the lush vegetation, especially in spring, and last but not least the monuments, make Qal'at Sim'an a popular excursion centre.*

QAL'AT SIM'AN. *The octagon of the great pilgrimage church, in the centre of which are the remains of the pillar on which St. Simeon lived. The socle and part of the lower pillar drum remain. There are said to have been three tambours, which symbolised the Holy Trinity.*

DAMASCUS. *As the western portico of the Omayyad mosque shows, the heritage of antiquity and Islamic tradition were combined here. On this basis Islamic architects achieved results which are admired all over the world.*

DAMASCUS. *The Omayyad mosque built in the 8th century, one of the most magnificent works of the early Islamic period, included ancient architectural elements. The so-called treasury in the northwest corner of the courtyard stands on pillars with Corinthian capitals.*

When the Roman Empire was divided into a Western and Eastern Empire in 395 A.D. Syria fell to the Eastern Roman Empire whose capital was Byzantium—Constantinople. It remained in the oriental diocese set up by the Emperor Diocletian in the 3rd century but was further divided for administrative purposes. Syria, the region west of the middle Euphrates, played an important part in the Byzantine state, which had the Roman law, Christian religion and Greek language. For the most part spared by enemy attacks during the 5th century, the country developed into a centre of Christian culture, with Christianity having taken root early in the towns. Differences from the Western Roman Empire increased, after the 6th century being evident in art, too. Independent developments in Syria were also furthered by the fact that the Syrian Christian church broke more and more away from the Orthodox Church of Byzantium after the 5th century. Although the church did not remain unified in Syria, but was divided confessionally into Monophysites and Nestorians, the church language was Syrian, while Greek was used in Byzantium. Syrian is an East Aramaic, i.e., Semitic tongue, of which there is written evidence from the 1st century A.D. onwards and in which an extensive literature was written and handed down. But it should be stressed that not all of Syria was involved in this development at the same time or to the same extent. The population, a large proportion of whom were Arabs, were partly Christian, but also worshipped the old Semitic gods. In many places the Christian religion and culture was mainly restricted to the towns.

The population of the towns were able to express themselves in art, especially architecture, to a greater extent than the broad masses. The Christian church and rich Christians were the actual commissioners of the architects, building artisans and artists of the period, so that it is not surprising that a number of Christian architectural monuments and single finds (cf. Page 177) of the Byzantine period have come down to us. During the two and a half centuries preceding the Islamic Arab conquest, numerous churches, baptisteries, martyries and monasteries were built. They are to be found in the Hauran region, in the oasis of Damascus, on the Euphrates and especially in North Syria. We mention here only the palace and basilica of Qasr ibn Wardan, northeast of Hama, el-Anderin (Androna), somewhat to the northeast of Qasr ibn Wardan, Ruweha with its two churches northeast of Ma'arret en-Nom'an, east of it the widespread ruins of el-Bara with its pyramid-shaped burial monuments, the magnificent basilica of Qalb Loze and the ruins of the monastery of Qasr el-Benat, not far from the Turkish frontier. A considerable proportion of these Christian buildings date from the time when the Byzantine Empire flourished under Emperor Justinian I (527–565). Two ruined sites of the Byzantine period are especially impressive: Rusafa and Qal'at Sim'an.

SERGIOPOLIS (RUSAFA)

Rusafa (also Rosapha, Resafa, Rosafa) is situated 26 km distant from the middle reaches of the Euphrates in the rolling landscape of the Syrian desert. The place was apparently already inhabited in ancient oriental times and was a stopping-place on the way from the Euphrates to Tadmur and farther into the cultivated part of Syria. In Graeco-Roman times it was a stopping-place between Sura (el-Hammam) on the Euphrates and Palmyra, and the limes built by the Emperor Diocletian touched it, as it did Palmyra. Since the surroundings of Rusafa, which was already known by this name in ancient oriental times, could hardly be used for agriculture, trade and the local market with the nomad tribes remained the basis of its existence. But it gained importance as a result of an event which took place under the Emperor Diocletian: Sergius, an Imperial palace official, was executed in Rusafa because of his steadfast adherence to Christianity and was buried there in 305. He is said to have refused to offer up sacrifices to Jupiter. Sergius' martyr's grave became famous throughout the Syrian desert and miracles which the dead man was supposed to have worked on pilgrims caused many more to make pilgrimages to it. Before the middle of the 5th century Rusafa became the seat of a bishopric and under the Emperor Anastasios (491–518) it was re-named Sergiopolis in honour of the saint.

The inhabitants of the city were mainly Arabs. To protect the place and the kingdom, a Byzantine garrison was stationed there, which on several occasions succeeded in resisting the attacks of the Persians. The city's wealth, based on sacrificial offerings and donations by believers, attracted armies in search of booty as well as pilgrims. Rusafa—the old name asserted itself again and again over the names Sergiopolis and Anastasiopolis—was expanded under the Emperor Justinian I (527–565), and was finally plundered by troops of the Persian King Chosrau II in 616. In the 8th century a violent

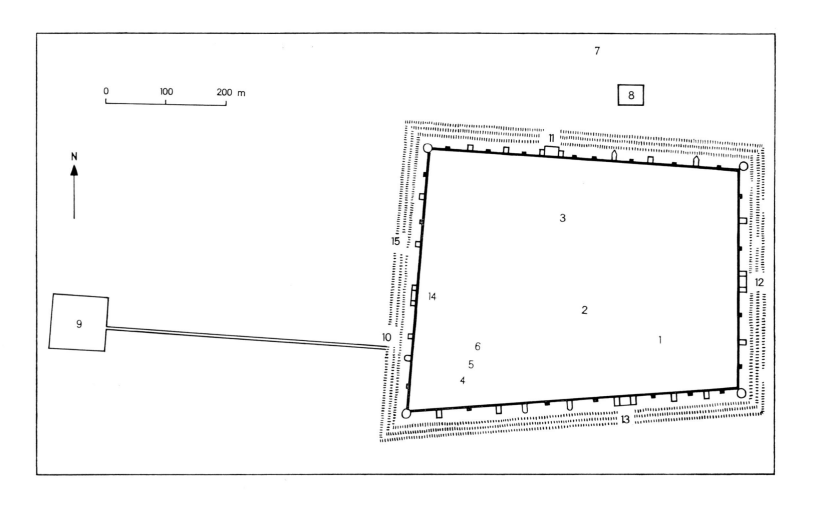

The main antique (Byzantine) buildings:

1 Sergius Basilica
2 "Basilica B"
3 Martyry
4 Big cistern
5 Small cistern
6 Small cistern
7 Burial church

8 Small water reservoir
9 Big water reservoir
10 Aqueduct
11 North gate
12 East gate
13 South gate
14 West gate
15 Ditch and city wall

SERGIOPOLIS. *Simplified over all plan after H. Spanner—S. Guyer, Rusafa. Die Wallfahrts-stadt des Heiligen Sergios (Berlin 1926), Plate 1.*

earthquake shook the city, but it was rebuilt by Caliph Hisham of the Omayyad dynasty, who resided in Damascus; the Caliph even had a palace built there. Rusafa now experienced another golden age which continued after the Omayyads were defeated and the Caliph's residence removed to Baghdad. But the situation in the Arab kingdom caused it to decline more and more until life died out in the second half of the 13th century—perhaps influenced by the Mongol invasion of 1260. Sultan Baibars (1260–1277) caused the few remaining inhabitants of Rusafa to be re-settled in the region of Hama in Central Syria; the place was last mentioned in 1283. After that no more was heard of this holy city in the desert. Its ruins were used from time to time as resting place by nomad tribes, and in modern times by the 'Aneze Bedouins.

News of the ruins reached Europe again only at the end of the 17th century, when English merchants travelling from Aleppo to Palmyra re-discovered them. Scholars like F. Sarre, E. Herzfeld, H. Spanner and S. Guyer have done especially good work in making the ruins accessible, and after 1952 a West German expedition under J. Kollwitz worked at Rusafa.

Approaching the ruins from the Euphrates along the road—which is in very good repair in dry weather—the traveller already sees the surrounding wall of the city from a considerable distance—"one of the best preserved examples of Byzantine fortress architecture" (S. Guyer). The walls surround an almost rectangular area with the corners facing the four points of the compass. J. Kollwitz' expedition measured the exact lengths of the walls: the south wall is 549.4 m, the

SERGIOPOLIS. *Basilica of Sergius. Reconstruction sketch by W. Beck, in: H. Spanner—S. Guyer, ibid., Plate 16.*

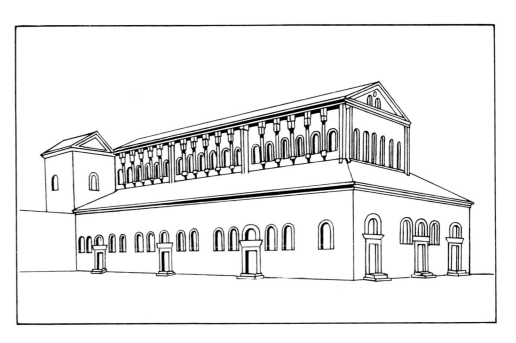

QAL'AT SIM'AN. *Complete ground plan after M. de Vogué, supplemented by D. Krencker with the help of aerial photos by G. Khalenko. After D. Krencker, Die Wallfahrtskirche des Simeon Stylites in Kal'at Sim'an (Berlin 1939), Plate 1.*

1 Octagonal building with Simeon's pillar
2 East basilica
3 North basilica
4 West basilica
5 South basilica
6 Portal (narthex)
7 Monastery courtyard
8 Monastery
9 Main entrance
10 Baptistery

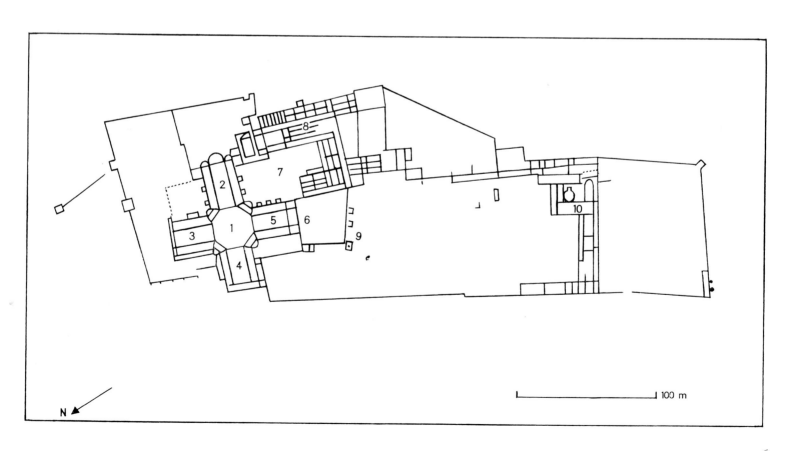

north wall 536.5 m, the west wall 411.2 m and the east wall 350.35 m in length. The area is thus an irregular rectangle. The walls originally rose to a height of 10 to 12 m and on the inner side there were defence passages, one in the middle of the wall and another above it. There were also curtains and towers for purposes of better defence, the towers protruding a considerable distance from the wall and built in a variety of shapes. In front of the wall there was a ditch and an earthen dam, traces of which can still be detected.

Four gates gave access to the city, one in the middle of each wall. The north gate is especially noteworthy *(Pages 180, 181)*. The most important street—leading to the Euphrates—left the city through this gate. It was richly ornamented, in accordance with its importance. Entering the city itself, which slopes slightly upwards to the east, one faces a broad area covered with the remains of Byzantine and Islamic buildings. It is covered with crater-like hollows where buildings collapsed and the local population plundered the ruins *(Page 178)*. These buildings were all built of white gypsum, dazzling in the sunshine, which obviously came from a quarry still recognisable today, situated somewhat north of the city.

Certainly the most important building within the walls of Rusafa is the Sergius Basilica *(Pages 179, 185)*. It probably dates from the turn of the 5th and 6th centuries, from the time when the place was named a metropolis by the Byzantine Emperor Anastasios and expanded. The basilica is in the southeastern part of the city, at the most elevated point. It is a three-aisle building with a transverse entrance hall; the apse is at the eastern end of the central aisle. The side aisles and the hall had a shed-roof and the central aisle a saddle-back roof. Inside, arches rest on pillars with Byzantine capitals and these separate the central from the side aisles. The central aisle is lit by big round-arched windows. Investigations have revealed that the church once had a second storey which could be reached by a winding stairway. A portico was built on to the west and south of the basilica at a later date.

Not far from the Sergius Basilica, which is probably the oldest church in this pilgrims' centre, lie the ruins of a building which is generally known as Basilica B *(Page 1)*. It was probably consecrated about the middle of the 6th century, perhaps in connection with the building activities going on in Rusafa under the Emperor Justinian I. The martyry near the north gate probably dates from about the same time and, like the gate itself, it still shows signs of rich architectonic decoration *(Page 182)*. Mention should finally be made of a church outside the city walls and of the Palace of Hisham built under Omayyad rule.

Three big underground structures in the southwest part of the city are of special interest. These were very probably cisterns for storing rainwater; the largest of them was certainly for this purpose. Water supply was the main problem in this city visited by crowds of pilgrims, for unlike Palmyra it had no springs. The ground water lies very deep here—more than 70 m below the surface. Since the transport of water from the Euphrates was expensive, rainwater was collected outside the city in reservoirs and conducted into it; the remains of an aqueduct laid over the defence ditch have survived. The big cistern to which rainwater was conducted measures 57.5 by 21.5 m and when it was completely full the water was 13 m deep, so that its total capacity was 15,000 to 16,000 cubic m. It is doubtful whether the winter rains were sufficient to provide this quantity of water. This huge space is divided into two parts by means of a thick wall broken by arches below and roofed over by barrel vaulting. The water was drawn in pails let down on ropes from a transverse room.

Rusafa, the white pilgrims' city in the Syrian desert, is without doubt one of the most interesting and most beautiful ruins of pre-Islamic Syria.

QAL'AT SIM'AN

We conclude our survey of ancient monuments of the Syrian Arab Republic not with city ruins but with those of a Christian monastery which was a place of pilgrimage—Saint Simeon or, as it is now called, Simeon's Fortress (Qal'at Sim'an).

The number of monks in Christian Syria increased in the 4th century. An especially characteristic and exaggerated kind of asceticism developed here—that of the Stylites. The founder of this sect was a monk called Simeon, who was born in 390 and later had a pillar erected on which he lived for about thirty years. He exercised a great influence on Christian Syria through his sermons delivered to listeners gathered at the foot of the pillar, but also through his letters. When Simeon Stylites (Simeon the Pillar Saint) died in 459 he was first buried on the pillar, but his corpse was taken to Antioch, the seat of the Patriarch, later on. However, the place where he had lived continued to be revered by the Christian population and there were many imitators of Simeon the Elder until well into the 10th century. A monastery named after Saint Simeon was built round the pillar in the 5th century.

Qal'at Sim'an lies northwest of Aleppo on a mountain ridge which commands a broad view over the valley of the river 'Afrin. The entire compound, which covers an area of about 12,000 square metres, is surrounded by a wall—like a fortress. Another wall separated the monastery itself—with the main building of Qual'at Sim'an, the great pilgrimage church—from the rest of the site. The Church of St. Simeon Stylites is a cross-shaped structure with a maximum length of 100 m. It actually consists of four churches and a central building. Dating back to the end of the 5th century, it can certainly be regarded as the finest Christian building of the Byzantine period in the whole of the Near East *(Page 188)*. The remains of the pillar on which Simeon once lived and preached forms the centre. This pillar, of which only the socle and part of the lower pillar drum remain today, was built up in the course of time to a height of 21 m. Around it was set up an octagonal building with big arches, which was transformed almost into a square by four apsidioles *(Page 189)* and opened into church buildings on four sides *(Pages 186, 187)*. There appear to be some grounds for assuming that the central building was not an open courtyard but was roofed by a wooden dome. The four adjacent three-aisled churches vary in architectural form. The biggest of them is the east basilica *(Page 187)*, whose eastern end has a main and two side apses. The three other churches, the north, west and south basilicas, are simpl-

QAL'AT SIM'AN. *Reconstruction of the original structure of the pilgrimage church. After D. Krencker, ibid., Plate 10.*

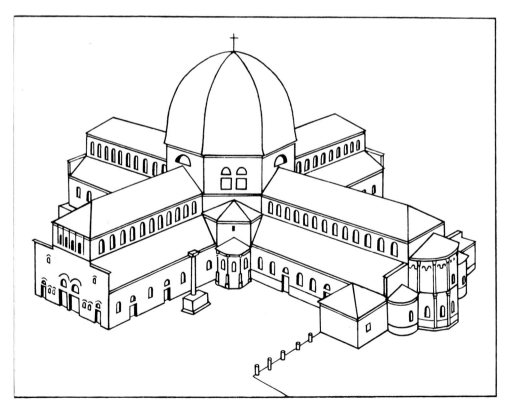

er in form. In front of the south basilica, towards the main entrance to the monastery compound, lies a richly decorated portal (narthex) with a main and two side entrances (Pages 183, 184). This may have been added in the 6th century. The monastery courtyard, followed by the monastery itself with a small church, adjoins the east and south basilicas. The baptistery is another building worthy of mention here; it is situated about 200 m south of the main church (Page 184). This is a square building combined with a three-aisle basilica. South of the church a gate in the outer wall leads to the road to Telanissos (today Der Sim'an) at the foot of Qal'at Sim'an. There are also numerous remains of Byzantine architecture in Der Sim'an, which once sheltered pilgrims to the monastery with Simeon's pillar. Large crowds of believers and other inquisitive people must have walked from here to the pillar of the saint in the days when Qal'at Sim'an flourished.

The Eastern Roman–Byzantine era came to an end in Syria about the middle of the 7th century. The decisive attacks by Islamic Arabs began in 633 and by 640 they had conquered the whole of Syria west of the Euphrates. Even before the middle of the century Mesopotamia, too, lay at the feet of the followers of the Prophet Mohammed. In 661 the Omayyad Caliphate was set up with Damascus as its capital and Syria was the centre of Islamic power until the fall of the Omayyads in 750. While the Arab element had already played an important role in the melting-pot Syria for a long period of time, Arabisation increased with the expansion of Islam. The Arab conquerors could link up with old tra-

ditions and they also adopted and preserved the treasures of antiquity (Page 190). Ancient traditions were taken into account in building Arab palaces and mosques, and architectural elements incorporated in them (Page 191). This can be seen in many places, the best-known example being the Omayyad mosque in Damascus, built in the early 8th century.

The heritage of ancient Syria has lived on under Islamic rule right down to our own times. It was not only the basis for the great achievements of Islamic-Arab architecture and science; it also continues to have its effect today as a factor not to be under-estimated in the development of a national historical concept. The people of the Syrian Arab Republic are deliberately taking possession of their past.

They have discovered more monuments of Syrian antiquity and are preserving them in museums (Page 192) and also where they were originally built, in their national surroundings.

SELECTED SOURCES

AMBRIÈRE, F., Editor. Die blauen Führer. Mittlerer Osten. Paris 1966 (Reiseführer).

ASSA'AD, KH., TAHA, O., Welcome to Palmyra. Damascus 1966.

BRÜNNOW, R.E., VON DOMASZEWSKI, A., Die Provincia Arabia, Vol. 3, Strasbourg 1909.

BUTLER, H.C., Southern Syria, in: Syria. Publications of the Princeton University Archaeological Expeditions to Syria in 1904–5 and 1909, Div. II: Architecture, Leyden 1919.

CUMONT, F., Fouilles de Dura Europos. Paris 1926.

DUNAND, M., SALIBY, N., Le Sanctuaire d'Amrit, in: Annales Archéologiques de Syrie 11–12 (1961–2), 3 et seq.

DUSSAUD, R., La pénétration des Arabes en Syrie avant l'Islam. Paris 1955.

HEICHELHEIM, F.M., Geschichte Syriens und Palästinas von der Eroberung durch Kyros II. bis zur Besitznahme durch den Islam, in: Handbuch der Orientalistik, I.2. IV.2, Leyden–Cologne 1966, 99 et seq.

HITTI, PH.K., History of Syria including Lebanon and Palestine. London 1957.

HONIGMANN, E., Syria, in: Real-Enzyklopaedie der klassischen Altertumswissenschaft, 1932, 1602 et seq.

KLENGEL, H., Geschichte und Kultur Altsyriens. Leipzig 1967.

KRENCKER, D., Die Wallfahrtskirche des Simeon Stylites in Kal'at Sim'an. Berlin 1939.

LACOSTE, H., La restitution du plan antique d'Apamée de Syrie, in: Bulletin de l'Académie Royale de Belgique, Classe des Beaux-Arts, 43 (1960), 53 et seq.

MATTERN, J., Villes mortes du Haute Syrie. Beirut 1944.

MICHAŁOWSKI, K., Palmyra. Warszawa 1968 (also Leipzig 1968).

PARROT, A., Mari. Munich 1953.

ROSTOVTZEFF, M.I., The Excavations at Dura Europos. New Haven 1929 et seq.

ROSTOVTZEFF, M.I., Dura Europos and its art. Oxford 1938.

SAUVAGET, J., Le plan antique de Damas, in: Syria 26 (1949), 314 et seq.

SCHAEFFER, CL.F.-A., Ugaritica. Paris 1939 et seq.

SPANNER, H., GUYER, S., Rusafa. Die Wallfahrtsstadt des Heiligen Sergios. Berlin 1926.

STARCKY, J., Palmyra. Paris 1952.

Università degli Studi di Roma. Missione archeologica in Siria. Rome 1965 et seq. (Tell Mardikh).

WIEGAND, TH. AND OTHERS. Palmyra. Die Ergebnisse der Expeditionen von 1902 und 1917. Berlin 1932.

SOURCE OF PHOTOGRAPHS

Aleppo, Museum: 42, 43, 44

Damascus, National Museum: 10, 26, 41, 43, 44, 45, 64, 67, 68, 69, 70, 71, 72, 79, 80, 92, 95, 96, 101, 111, 120, 129, 135, 136, 150, 164, 165, 166, 172, 182 (Most of the photographs are by M. Musselmani).

Hirmer Photo Archives, Munich: 3, 9, 12, 34, 37

Professor P. Matthiae, Rome: 17, 18

Coin Collection of the State Museums in Berlin: 110

Professor F. Sarre: 58, 66, 175, 176, 178, 180, 182 (Property of the Islamic Museum of the State Museums in Berlin)

All other photographs are by the author.